Blender 2.5 Lighting and Rendering

Bring your 3D world to life with lighting, compositing, and rendering

Aaron W. Powell

[PACKT] open source*
community experience distilled

PUBLISHING

BIRMINGHAM - MUMBAI

Blender 2.5 Lighting and Rendering

First published: November 2010

Production Reference: 2021110

Published by Packt Publishing Ltd.
32 Lincoln Road
Olton
Birmingham, B27 6PA, UK.

ISBN 978-1-847199-88-1

www.packtpub.com

Cover Image by Aaron Powell (aaron@cgshark.com)

Credits

Author
Aaron W. Powell

Reviewers
Yorik van Havre
Sanu Vamanchery Mana

Acquisition Editor
Sarah Cullington

Development Editor
Reshma Sundaresan

Technical Editor
Kartikey Pandey

Copy Editor
Leonard D'Silva

Indexers
Tejal Daruwale
Monica Ajmera Mehta

Editorial Team Leader
Mithun Sehgal

Project Team Leader
Lata Basantani

Project Coordinator
Leena Purkait

Proofreader
Aaron Nash

Production Coordinator
Kruthika Bangera

Cover Work
Kruthika Bangera

About the Author

Aaron Powell developed a passion for computer graphics early in his high school career. Developing "stick figure animations" using the primitive drawing tools of Microsoft PowerPoint, he quickly discovered he wanted to learn about other ways of using animation, always looking to broaden his scope. Tired of crashing PowerPoint, he soon stumbled upon the open source animation program Blender, and immediately got involved with the community that surrounded it. Since then, Aaron has worked as a freelance artist and tutor, focusing on lighting and rendering techniques in both Blender and Autodesk Maya.

He now attends the Rochester Institute of Technology, pursuing a degree in 3D Digital Graphics, meanwhile giving back to the Blender community through his efforts at CGShark.com. CGShark is an online blog that provides interesting news not only about Blender, but also about the computer graphics industry at large, including movie and book reviews, artist interviews, and other interesting "tid-bits" of information about computer graphics. The blog also proudly hosts Roland Hess's book, "The Essential Blender" as a free PDF download, which brings readers from beginner to computer graphics novice with Blender.

> This book is dedicated to my parents, Darryl and Holly, who have graciously supported me throughout this entire process, and to my professors at the Rochester Institute of Technology who dared to push me beyond what I thought I could do.

About the Reviewers

Yorik van Havre is a Belgian architect who currently lives and works in São Paulo, Brazil. Blender occupies the major part of his daily work. He regularly writes articles and tutorials about Blender, architecture and architecture software, and is actively involved in several communities and open-source projects. He has also reviewed two other Blender books, *Blender 3D: Architecture, Buildings and Scenery and Blender 3D Incredible machines*, both by Allan Brito. More about Yorik's work can be found at his website: http://yorik.uncreated.net

Sanu Vamanchery Mana is a 3D artist from India with over 11 years of experience in the fields of animation, gaming, and special effects, and is Lecturer of Interactive Media Design/Animation and Game Design at Raffles Design Institute, Singapore. As a lecturer he has given many workshops, trainings, and presentations in many countries in Europe, Asia, and Latin America. Currently he is reviewing two Blender 3D books for Packt Publishing.

He has worked for gaming projects such as Golden Eye 007 (Electronic Arts), Neopet (Sony Entertainment), and World Series of Poker (Sony Entertainment). He was also involved in the Short movie "JackFrost" was which nominated for a BAFTA.

Table of Contents

Preface

The field of lighting and rendering for computer graphics is a vast and extremely interesting one. Film and animation, game design, medical illustration, even set visualization for theatre—all of these require someone specialized in lighting to see a project to completion. One of the many appeals of lighting is the desire to recreate conditions found in the world around us. Our world is full of many interesting and unique environments, each with their own atmosphere and visual aesthetic. As we begin our endeavors into the field of lighting and rendering, we will take a look at three common lighting scenarios presented in computer graphics:

* Exterior environments
* Interior environments
* Lighting environments that incorporate both natural and artificial light sources (a mix of exterior and interior environments)

What this book covers

Chapter 1, Introduction to Color Theory and Lighting Basics in Blender, guides us to effectively use lights to create mood or to simulate a certain kind of environment in a 3D scene; we should have a solid understanding of how color theory works and how Blender treats light. This chapter introduces basic color theory, including color relationships, color temperature, and chromatic adaptation. We will then take a look at the different types of lights Blender provides as well as lighting "rigs" and how to set them up in Blender.

Chapter 2, Outdoor Lighting: Setting Up Our Scene, introduces Blender's Internal Renderer, as well as some important settings we need to know about before embarking on our lighting and rendering escapade. We also discuss the importance of developing and utilizing an efficient workflow when working on a project, and the questions we should ask ourselves before lighting a scene. After that, we'll proceed to set up a basic 3-Point light rig for our exterior scene.

Chapter 3, Ambient Lighting Techniques in Blender, examines how Blender uses ambient lighting, and the algorithms it provides, including ambient occlusion, Environment Lighting, and Indirect Lighting. Once we understand how ambient lighting works in Blender, we will apply it to our exterior scene.

Chapter 4, Outdoor Scene: Adding Materials, introduces Blender's materials and how to create them. It discusses many of the features that come along with materials as well, including color, textures, reflections, and transparency. After we understand how Blender handles materials, we'll create some for our exterior scene.

Chapter 5, Indoor Lighting: Setting Up, moves on to an interior scene after completing our exterior scene. We'll discuss some of the differences between the two environments and what to watch out for when lighting them. Following our workflow, we'll begin to set our lights, learning how to use Blender's 3D layers to create interesting effects with our light rig.

Chapter 6, UV Mapping and Texturing, discusses a concept called UV mapping and the tools Blender has to work with it. We'll also learn how to create a custom UV map and texture for an object in our interior scene.

Chapter 7, Indoor Lighting: Finishing Materials, takes a look at creating materials for the rest of our scene. We'll learn how to use Blender's Compositor to create materials, as well as how to create the illusion of depth-of-field blurring.

Chapter 8, Combining Indoor and Outdoor Lighting Techniques, introduces our final scenario: lighting a scene with both indoor and outdoor light sources. We'll discuss things to be aware of and how to approach a scene like this. Afterward, we will proceed to light our example scene.

Chapter 9, Hybrid Lighting: Materials and Textures, looks at how to create the materials and textures for our scene. These materials include concrete, wood, glass, metal, and more.

What you need for this book

In order to follow along with this book, you'll need to download the latest version of Blender (Blender v2.5), which can be downloaded for free at `http://www.blender.org`. For image editing, we will be using the GIMP, which can be downloaded for free at `http://www.gimp.org`, but you as the reader are free to use whatever image manipulation program you're comfortable with.

All project files that are needed for this book, including Blender files and texture files, can be downloaded from CGShark.com at `http://www.cgshark.com/lighting-and-rendering/`, or from the Packt Publishing website (`http://packtpub.com/support`).

Who this book is for

If you are a Blender user and you want to improve the quality of your renders, this book is for you. You need to have experience in Blender and know your way around the Blender interface. You may be a professional or freelancer or hobbyist willing to increase the quality of your portfolio and interested in adding perfection to your renders.

Conventions

In this book, you will find a number of styles of text that distinguish between different kinds of information. Here are some examples of these styles, and an explanation of their meaning.

Code words in text are shown as follows: "We select the `label_mask.png` image from the Interior Lighting project list."

New terms and **important words** are shown in bold. Words that you see on the screen, in menus or dialog boxes for example, appear in the text like this: "Under the **Influence settings**, uncheck the box next to **Color**, and check the box next to **Normal**".

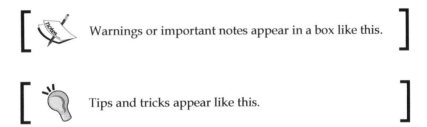

Warnings or important notes appear in a box like this.

Tips and tricks appear like this.

Reader feedback

Feedback from our readers is always welcome. Let us know what you think about this book—what you liked or may have disliked. Reader feedback is important for us to develop titles that you really get the most out of.

To send us general feedback, simply send an e-mail to `feedback@packtpub.com`, and mention the book title via the subject of your message.

If there is a book that you need and would like to see us publish, please send us a note in the **SUGGEST A TITLE** form on `www.packtpub.com` or e-mail `suggest@packtpub.com`.

If there is a topic that you have expertise in and you are interested in either writing or contributing to a book, see our author guide on `www.packtpub.com/authors`.

Customer support

Now that you are the proud owner of a Packt book, we have a number of things to help you to get the most from your purchase.

Downloading the example files for this book

You can download the example files for all Packt books you have purchased from your account at http://www.PacktPub.com. If you purchased this book elsewhere, you can visit http://www.PacktPub.com/support and register to have the files e-mailed directly to you.

Downloading the color images of this book

We also provide you a PDF file that has color images of the screenshots used in this book. The color images will help you better understand the changes in the output. You can download this file from https://www.packtpub.com/sites/default/files/9881_images.pdf

Errata

Although we have taken every care to ensure the accuracy of our content, mistakes do happen. If you find a mistake in one of our books—maybe a mistake in the text or the code—we would be grateful if you would report this to us. By doing so, you can save other readers from frustration and help us improve subsequent versions of this book. If you find any errata, please report them by visiting http://www.packtpub.com/support, selecting your book, clicking on the **errata submission form** link, and entering the details of your errata. Once your errata are verified, your submission will be accepted and the errata will be uploaded on our website, or added to any list of existing errata, under the Errata section of that title. Any existing errata can be viewed by selecting your title from http://www.packtpub.com/support.

Piracy

Piracy of copyright material on the Internet is an ongoing problem across all media. At Packt, we take the protection of our copyright and licenses very seriously. If you come across any illegal copies of our works, in any form, on the Internet, please provide us with the location address or website name immediately so that we can pursue a remedy.

Please contact us at copyright@packtpub.com with a link to the suspected pirated material.

We appreciate your help in protecting our authors, and our ability to bring you valuable content.

Questions

You can contact us at questions@packtpub.com if you are having a problem with any aspect of the book, and we will do our best to address it.

1
Introduction to Color Theory and Lighting Basics in Blender

Before we can recreate realistic lighting in any 3D application, we must first understand how color and light relate to each other and the world around them. The term "realistic lighting" doesn't just apply to natural light given off by the sun or moon—it also includes light given off by artificial sources including florescent lights, halogen lights, incandescent lights, and many other types of lights that are found in the world around us. It's important to understand not only how, but also why certain light sources behave as they do, so we can effectively apply the right lighting techniques to our 3D scenes.

To understand how light works, we're going to take a look at:

- Basic color theory and color relationships
- Color temperature
- Various light sources
- Chromatic adaptation
- Lamp types in Blender
- Components of a basic light rig
- Various light rigs and their implementation in Blender
- How Blender deals with shadows

Basic color theory

To fully understand how light works, we need to have a basic understanding of what color is and how different colors interact with each other. The study of this phenomenon is known as **color theory**.

What is color?

When light comes in contact with an object, the object absorbs a certain amount of that light. The rest is reflected into the eye of the viewer in the form of color. The easiest way to visualize colors and their relations is in the form of a **color wheel**.

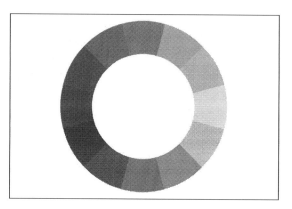

Primary colors

There are millions of colors, but there are only three colors that cannot be created through color mixing—red, yellow, and blue. These colors are known as primary colors, which are used to create the other colors on the color wheel through a process known as *color mixing*. Through color mixing, we get other "sets" of colors, including secondary and tertiary colors.

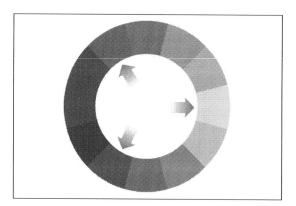

Secondary colors

Secondary colors are created when two primary colors are mixed together. For example, mixing red and blue makes purple, red and yellow make orange, and blue and yellow make green.

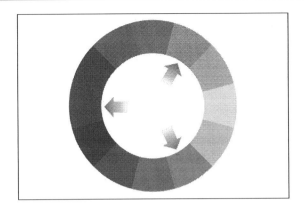

Tertiary colors

It's natural to assume that, because mixing two primary colors creates a secondary color, mixing two secondary colors would create a tertiary color. Surprisingly, this isn't the case. A tertiary color is, in fact, the result of mixing a primary and secondary color together. This gives us the remainder of the color wheel:

- Red-orange
- Orange-yellow
- Chartreuse
- Turquoise
- Indigo
- Violet-red

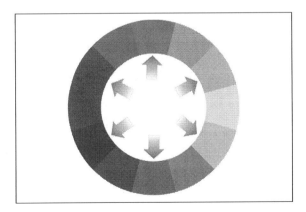

Color relationships

There are other relationships between colors that we should know about before we start using Blender. The first is **complimentary colors**. Complimentary colors are colors that are across from each other on the color wheel.

For example, red and green are compliments. Complimentary colors are especially useful for creating contrast in an image, because mixing them together darkens the hue. In a computer program, mixing perfect compliments together will result in black, but mixing compliments in a more traditional medium such as oil pastels results in more of a dark brown hue. In both situations, though, the compliments are used to create a darker value.

 Be wary of using complimentary colors in computer graphics—if complimentary colors mix accidentally, it will result in black artifacts in images or animations.

The other color relationship that we should be aware of is analogous colors. Analogous colors are colors found next to each other on the color wheel. For example, red, red-orange, and orange are analogous. Here's the kicker—red, orange, and yellow can also be analogous as well. A good rule to follow is as long as you don't span more than one primary color on the color wheel, they're most likely considered analogous colors.

Color temperature

Understanding color temperature is an essential step in understanding how lights work—at the very least, it helps us understand why certain lights emit the colors they do. No light source emits a constant light wavelength. Even the sun, although considered a *constant* light source, is filtered by the atmosphere to various degrees based on the time of the day, changing its perceived color.

Color temperature is typically measured in degrees Kelvin (°K), and has a color range from a red to blue hue, like in the image below:

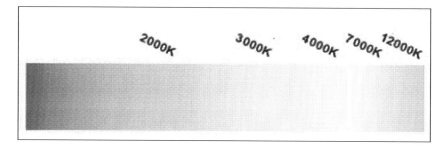

Every color in the temperature spectrum corresponds to a specific Kelvin value. Knowing this correlation will help us understand how real light sources work.

Real world, real lights

So how is color applicable beyond a two-dimensional color wheel? In the real world, our eyes perceive color because light from the sun—which contains all colors in the visible color spectrum—is reflected off of objects in our field of vision. As light hits an object, some wavelengths are absorbed, while the rest are reflected. Those reflected rays are what determine the color we perceive that particular object to be.

Of course, the sun isn't the only source of light we have. There are many different types of natural and artificial light sources, each with its own unique properties. The most common types of light sources we may try to simulate in Blender include:

- Candlelight
- Incandescent light
- Florescent light
- Sunlight
- Skylight

Candlelight

Candlelight is a source of light as old as time. It has been used for thousands of years and is still used today in many cases. The color temperature of a candle's light is about 1500 K, giving it a warm red-orange hue. Candlelight also has a tendency to create really high contrast between lit areas and unlit areas in a room, which creates a very successful dramatic effect.

Incandescent light bulbs

When most people hear the term "light bulb", the incandescent light bulb immediately comes to mind. It's also known as a tungsten-halogen light bulb. It's your typical household light bulb, burning at approximately 2800 K-3200 K. This color temperature value still allows it to fall within the orange-yellow part of the spectrum, but it is noticeably brighter than the light of a candle.

Florescent light bulbs

Florescent lights are an alternative to incandescent. Also known as mercury vapor lights, fluorescents burn at a color temperature range of 3500 K-5900 K, allowing them to emit a color anywhere between a yellow and a white hue. They're commonly used when lighting a large area effectively, such as a warehouse, school hallway, or even a conference room.

The sun and the sky

Now let's take a look at some natural sources of light! The most obvious example is the sun. The sun burns at a color temperature of approximately 5500 K, giving it its bright white color. We rarely use pure white as a light's color in 3D though—it makes your scene look too artificial. Instead, we may choose to use a color that best suits the scene at hand. For example, if we are lighting a desert scene, we may choose to use a beige color to simulate light bouncing off the sand. But even so, this still doesn't produce an entirely realistic effect. This is where the next source of light comes in—the sky.

The sky can produce an entire array of colors from deep purple to orange to bright blue. It produces a color temperature range of 6000 K-20,000 K. That's a huge range! We can really use this to our advantage in our 3D scenes—the color of the sky can have the final say in what the mood of your scene ends up being.

Chromatic adaptation

What is chromatic adaptation? We're all more familiar with this process than you may realize. As light changes, the color we perceive from the world around us changes. To accommodate for those changes, our eyes adjust what we see to something we're more familiar with (or what our brains would consider normal). When working in 3D you have to keep this in mind, because even though your 3D scene may be physically lit correctly, it may not look natural because the computer renders the final image objectively, without the chromatic adaptation that we, as humans, are used to.

Take this image for example. In the top image, the second card from the left appears to be a stronger shade of pink than the corresponding card in the bottom picture. Believe it or not, they are the exact same color, but because of the red hue of the second photo, our brains change how we perceive that image.

Lighting basics in Blender

Now that we have a basic understanding of real-world light sources and color theory, we can start applying it to our 3D scenes. Let's take a look at the lamp types found in Blender, some basic lighting setups (or "rigs"), and how Blender deals with shadows.

Blender provides us with five different types of lamps we can use to light our scenes:

- Point
- Sun
- Spot
- Hemi
- Area

These lamps can be added to a scene through the **Add** menu.

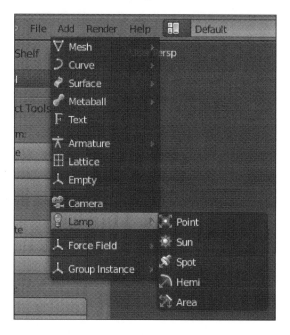

The Point lamp

When we open Blender for the first time, the default scene includes a cube, a camera, and a Point lamp.

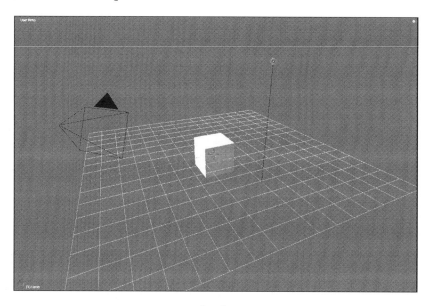

The Point lamp is an omni-directional light, meaning it emits light in all directions. There is, as with all other lamps in Blender, a fall-off factor, which means that as the distance between an object and the light source increases, the amount of light illuminating the object decreases.

The Sun lamp

The sun is so far away from earth that as light rays travel away from the sun, the angle between them grows closer and closer to 0. Because of this phenomenon, a convention in the CG industry is to simulate sunlight with a lamp that emits light in a single direction with parallel rays.

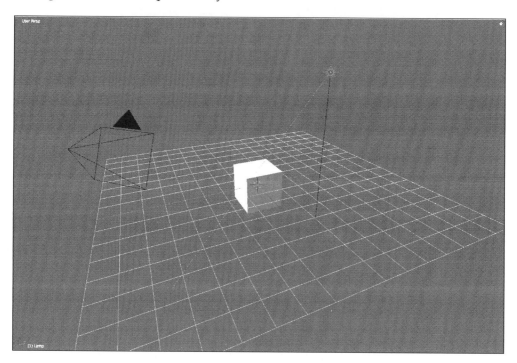

Other 3D programs refer to this lamp as a "direction light", but they all behave in the same fashion.

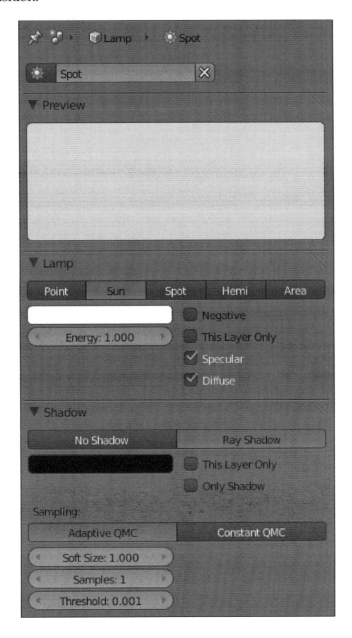

The Spot lamp

The Spot lamp acts in the same fashion a spot light would in the real world. When we break it down, the Spot lamp is a default lamp attached to a cone, restricting the light to the volume of the cone. The settings for the size and length of the cone can be edited manually to fit different needs.

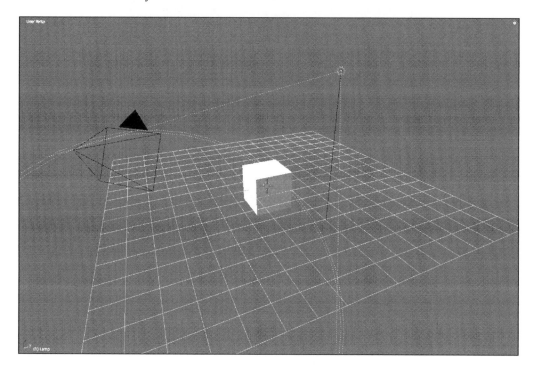

This lamp is especially useful for scenes that require large contrasts in light such as scenes using a 1-Point light rig (we will discuss this later). A nice feature that sets it apart from some of the other lights is that the Spot lamp supports both buffer and raytraced shadows—some of the other lamp types only support raytraced shadows. For more information on the difference between Blender's shadow algorithms, refer to the *Shadows* section at the end of this chapter.

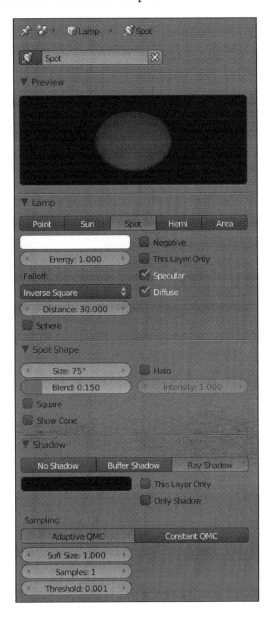

The Hemi lamp

The Hemi lamp directs light by emitting light in one direction from a hemispherical shape. Sounds confusing? It works in the same way the flash from an old camera would, used to simulate a cloudy (or otherwise uniform) sky.

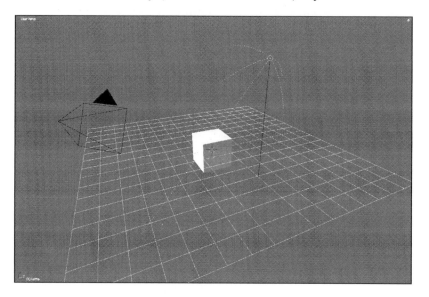

Just like the Sun lamp, the direction of the Hemi lamp is only affected by the lamp's rotation, and not its position.

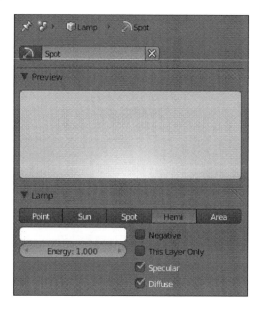

Area lamp

The Area lamp is an interesting lamp. All of the other lamps in Blender are single-point lamps, meaning they light a scene based on light rays emitted from a single point.

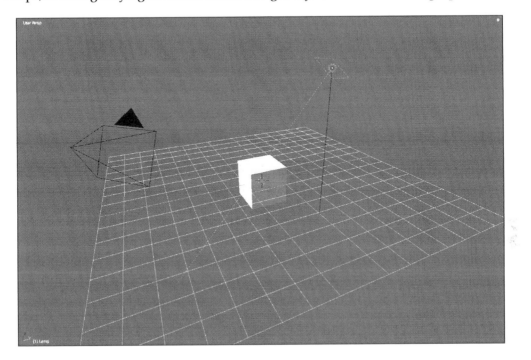

The Area lamp is different in that it's a multi-point light. This means that when it comes to render an image, Blender places a user-determined number of point lights within the boundaries of the Area lamp and then calculates the effect those lights have on the scene. This creates smoother shadows, and emulates the effect of *bending* light.

Of course, this algorithm does have some rendering consequences. The first, and most obvious one, is that the number of lamps used in the Area lamp multiplies the time it takes Blender to render the image. Secondly, some objects will not receive the full effect of the Area lamp due to other objects blocking the rays from some of the Blender-generated lights. Placing several lamps on a grid can create the same effect, but the Area lamp gives you more precise control over shadow settings and other parameters.

Basic light rigs

Now that we understand how lamps in Blender work, we can arrange them in our scenes in formations known as "light rigs". There are many ways to set up a rig, but the most commonly used rigs consist of three parts:

- Key light
- Fill light
- Backlight

The key light is the main light source in a composition. More often than not, it's used to light most of the object (or objects) in question as well as define the overall color that light will produce in the scene.

Manish Bansal http://www.flickr.com/photos/bansal98/4082969879/

The fill light works with the key light, lighting some of the darker areas of the image created by the key light.

Anthony Kelly http://www.flickr.com/photos/62337512@N00/2419509840/

The backlight—also known as a rim light—is useful for distinguishing objects in the foreground from the background of the image. It creates a rim of light on the edges of objects, giving them another level of dimensionality.

Stephan Mantler http://www.flickr.com/photos/stepman/4323534986/

1-Point light rig

The first rig we'll take a look at is a 1-Point light rig. This is the simplest type of light rig, using only a single light, the key light, to illuminate a scene.

Many times, a Spot lamp is used with this rig, producing an image with sharp contrast between light and dark areas.

2-Point light rig

The next rig is a 2-Point light rig. Consisting of a key and fill light, this rig is typically used when you want to evenly illuminate a scene (mostly if there is no main focus). It's actually not uncommon for photography studios to use a tangible adaptation of this rig to light a product for a company.

The key light and fill light are typically placed on opposite sides of the camera, slighting above the scene and oriented toward the object in question. This gives the even lighting this rig is known for.

3-Point light rig

The 3-Point light rig is one of the most commonly used templates for lighting scenes. The construction of this rig differs depending on who is constructing it, but there are two "standard templates" that appear often in CG lighting, namely, the Studio rig and the Standard rig.

The Studio rig consists of a key light and two fill lights. The fill lights are typically placed on the side of the scene opposite the key light, illuminating the object from behind.

The Standard rig differs from studio to studio, but the overall idea remains the same. I personally set up a Standard rig with a key light, a backlight, and a sidelight. The key light, of course, is the brightest, positioned above, in front, and to the side of the object. The backlight is less intense as compared to the key light and is positioned closer to the ground behind the object. The fill light is off to the side, opposite the key light.

4-Point light rig

The last type of lighting rig we are going to look at is the 4-Point lighting rig.

This rig provides a good simulation of outside lighting—it's basically a hybrid of the Studio and Standard 3-Point lighting rigs. A key light illuminates the scene with the help of two fill lights off to each side. A backlight helps distinguish the background from the foreground.

Shadows

Blender approaches shadows in two ways. The first is with raytracing. Raytraced shadows are mathematically correct, but they take longer to render. They're calculated by projecting rays of "light" from a light source and using the direction of those rays to create the shadow. The other type of shadow in Blender is called a **buffer shadow**. Buffer shadows are rendered much faster than raytraced shadows, but at the cost of quality and buffer memory.

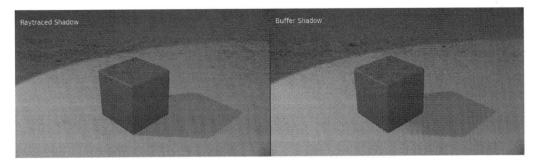

Summary

We've learned a lot about real-world light sources and their properties. We've also taken a look at color theory—both of these subjects are going to prove essential to the rest of this book. In addition, we've taken a look at Blender's native light types and how to arrange them to effectively achieve various results within our 3D scene. Let's take a look at what we've covered so far:

- Color is the light reflected off objects
- Color temperature is the "temperature" of the perceived light in degrees Kelvin
- There are many different kinds of natural and artificial lights, each with their own distinct characteristics
- Blender has many internal light types, each with its own unique properties
- To effectively light a 3D scene, you can employ various light "rigs", including 1, 2, 3, and 4-Point lighting rigs
- Blender deals with shadows in various ways—depending on your scene or budget, you may choose one technique over the other

2
Outdoor Lighting: Setting Up Our Scene

Lighting techniques are highly dependent on the location of the scene at hand. The approaches to lighting an outdoor scene are radically different from the techniques used to light an indoor scene. Knowing these differences and when to use each is important when aiming for a believable result. We will take a look at:

- Establishing a workflow
- Things to consider when lighting a scene
- Adding and editing lights in Blender
- How to use layers to increase the quality of our render
- What habits are good when lighting and why

Getting the right files

Before we get started, we need a scene to work with. There are three scenes provided for our use—an outdoor scene, an indoor scene, and a hybrid scene that incorporates elements that are found both inside as well as outside. All these files can be downloaded from `http://www.cgshark.com/lighting-and-rendering/`.

The file we are going to use for this scene is called `exterior.blend`. This scene contains a tricycle, which we will light as if it were a product being promoted for a company.

 To download the files for this tutorial, visit `http://www.cgshark.com/lighting-and-rendering/` and select `exterior.blend`.

Blender render settings

In computer graphics, a two-dimensional image is created from three-dimensional data through a computational process known as **rendering**. It's important to understand how to customize Blender's internal renderer settings to produce a final result that's optimized for our project, be it a single image or a full-length film. With the settings Blender provides us, we can set frame rates for animation, image quality, image resolution, and many other essential parts needed to produce that optimized final result. Because we are going to use the same render settings for all projects in this book, we are going to take a look at how to set those values now.

The Scene menu

We can access these render settings through the **Scene** menu. Here, we can adjust a myriad of settings. For the sake of these projects, we are only going to be concerned with:

- Which window Blender will render our image in
- How render layers are set up (we will discuss this in more detail later on)
- Image dimensions
- Output location and file type

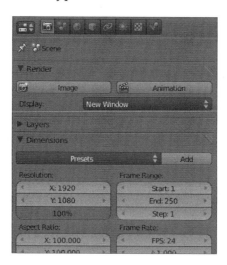

Render settings

The first settings we see when we look at the **Scene** menu are the **Render** settings. Here, we can tell Blender to render the current frame or an animation using the render buttons.

We can also choose what type of window we want Blender to render our image in using the **Display** options.

The first option (and the one chosen by default) is **Full Screen**. This renders our image in a window that overlaps the three-dimensional window in our scene. To restore the three-dimensional view, select the **Back to Previous** button at the top of the window.

The next option is the **Image Editor** that Blender uses both for rendering as well as UV editing, which we will cover later. This is especially useful when using the Compositor, allowing us to see our result alongside our composite node setup. By default, Blender replaces the three-dimensional window with the Image Editor.

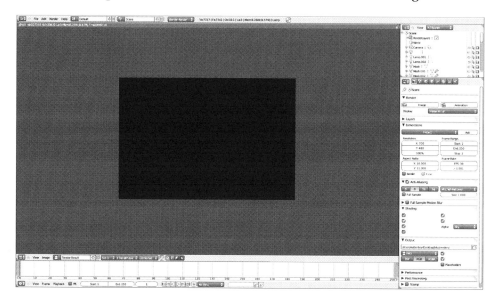

The last option is the option that Blender has used, by default, since day one—**New Window**. This means that Blender will render the image in a newly created window, separate from the rest of the program's interface.

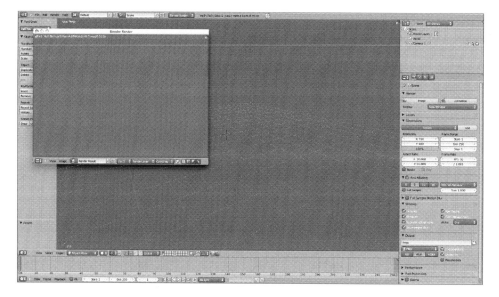

For the sake of these projects, we're going to keep this setting at the default setting—**Full Screen**.

Dimensions settings

These are some of the most important settings that we can set when dealing with optimizing our project output. We can set the image size, frame rate, frame range, and aspect ratio of our render. Luckily for us, Blender provides us with preset render settings, common in the film industry:

- HDTV 1080P
- HDTV 720P
- TV NTSC
- TV PAL
- TV PAL 16:9

Because we want to keep our render times relatively low for our projects, we're going to set our preset dimensions to TV NTSC, which results in an image 720 pixels wide by 480 pixels high. If you're interested in learning more about how the other formats behave, feel free to visit `http://en.wikipedia.org/wiki/Display_resolution`.

Output settings

These settings are an important factor when determining how we want our final product to be viewed. Blender provides us with numerous image and video types to choose from.

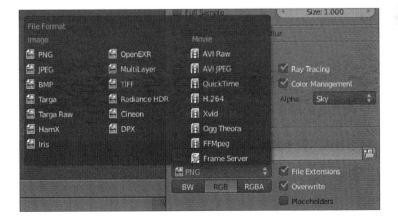

When rendering an animation or image sequence, it's always easier to manually set the folder we want Blender to save to. We can tell Blender where we want it to save by establishing the path in the output settings. By default on Macintosh, Blender saves to the /tmp/ folder.

Now that we understand how Blender's renderer works, we can start working with our scene!

Establishing a workflow

The key to constantly producing high-quality work is to establish a well-tested and efficient workflow. Everybody's workflow is different, but over the course of the next few chapters, we are going to follow this series of steps:

1. Evaluate what the scene we are lighting will require.
2. Plan how we want to lay out the lamps in our scene.
3. Set lamp positions, intensities, colors, and shadows, if applicable.
4. Add materials and textures.
5. Tweak until we're satisfied.

Evaluating our scene

Before we even begin to approach a computer, we need to think about our scene from a conceptual perspective. This is important, because knowing everything about our scene and the story that's taking place will help us produce a more realistic result.

To help kick start this process, we can ask ourselves a series of questions that will get us thinking about what's happening in our scene. These questions can pertain to an entire array of possibilities and conditions, including:

- Weather
  - What is the weather like on this particular day? What was it like the day before or the day after?
  - Is it cloudy, sunny, or overcast? Did it rain or snow?
- Source of light
  - Where is the light coming from? Is it in front of, to the side, or even behind the object?

- ○ Remember, light is reflected and refracted until all energy is absorbed; this not only affects the color of the light, but the quality as well. Do we need to add additional light sources to simulate this effect?

- Scale of light sources

  - ○ What is the scale of our light sources in relation to our three-dimensional scene? Believe it or not, this factor carries a lot of weight when it comes to the quality of the final render. If any lights feel out of place, it could potentially affect the believability of the final product.

The goal of these questions is to prove to ourselves that the scene we're lighting has the potential to exist in real life. It's much harder, if not impossible, to light a scene if we don't know how it could possibly act in the real world.

Let's take a look at these questions.

- **What is the weather like?** In our case, we're not concerned with anything too challenging, weather wise. The goal of this tutorial is to depict our tricycle in an environment that reflects the effects of a sunny, cloudless day. To achieve this, we are going to use lights with blue and yellow hues for simulating the effect the sun and sky will have on our tricycle.

- **What are the sources of our light and where are they coming from in relation to our scene?** In a real situation, the sun would provide most of the light, so we'll need a key light that simulates how the sun works. In our case, we can use a Sun lamp. The key to positioning light sources within a three-dimensional scene is to find a compromise between achieving the desired mood of the image and effectively illuminating the object being presented.

- **What is the scale of our light sources?** The sun is rather large, but because of the nature of the Sun lamp in Blender, we don't have to worry about the scale of the lamp in our three-dimensional scene. Sometimes—more commonly when working with indoor scenes, such as the scene we'll approach later—certain light sources need to be of certain sizes in relation to our scene, otherwise the final result will feel unnatural.

Although we will be using a realistic approach to materials, textures, and lighting, we are going to present this scene as a product visualization. This means that we won't explicitly show a ground plane, allowing the viewer to focus on the product being presented, in this case, our tricycle.

Planning our light rig

Knowing that our scene has the potential to really exist somewhere in the real world, we can now plan how we want to set up our lamps within Blender to produce a realistic result.

The first step in this process is to choose an appropriate light rig. Think about the mood we want to create and the environment our scene contains—do we need harsh lighting with sharp shadows, or maybe something more evenly lit? Once we know what we want, we can choose between any of the light rigs we learned about in *Chapter 1, Introduction to Color Theory and Lighting Basics in Blender*. Remember, these options include:

- 1-Point light rig
- 2-Point light rig
- 3-Point light rig
- 4-Point light rig

Sometimes, we'll light scenes that require a combination of light rigs. If that's the case, try to imagine how lights would be set up in a real situation to create the effect we want to reproduce.

We should also think about what lamps we should use in our rigs. Remember, each lamp type in Blender has its own unique qualities and will simulate some types of real-world light sources better than others will. The types we can choose from, as seen in the previous chapter, are:

- Point lamp
- Sun lamp
- Spot lamp
- Hemi lamp
- Area lamp

For this particular scene, we are going to use a 3-Point light rig. If needed, we'll add a fourth later. The 3-Point light rig is appropriate for two main reasons:

- This is an outdoor scene. In a natural setting, light would be illuminating our object from every angle. The 3-Point lighting rig can simulate this phenomenon, and when properly set up, will effectively illuminate our object without a problem.

- We are promoting a product, in our case, a tricycle. When working with scenes of this nature, it is a good practice to light objects from multiple angles to best advertise the product or service being advertised.

In addition, fill and rim lights will help increase the perceived dimensionality of our three-dimensional objects, simulating the effect of light reflection and refraction.

Setting up our scene

We've conceptually developed our scene and created a light setup that will realistically reflect how our tricycle could possibly be lit in the real world. Now we can open our three-dimensional file and physically begin positioning lamps in Blender.

Wolfgang Staudt `http://www.flickr.com/photos/wolfgangstaudt/640522931/`

This is where our knowledge of color theory will come in handy. For example, if our scene takes place in a park, we may use blue, yellow, and green hues to reflect the color of light given off by the sun, sky, and grass.

"Theopie" `http://www.flickr.com/photos/opie/916777666/`

On the other end of the scale, if our scene takes place in a dark setting, such as a bar, we may choose to use colors like red, brown, green, and/or purple to simulate the colors created by the wood of the bar itself, the colors of the bar stools, or the colors of the neon sign flashing in the window. You may even include a blue light to simulate the flickering street lamp across the street.

When you open your scene for the first time, you should see something similar to the following image. If you don't, make sure you download the right file from the website http://www.cgshark.com/lighting-and-rendering/.

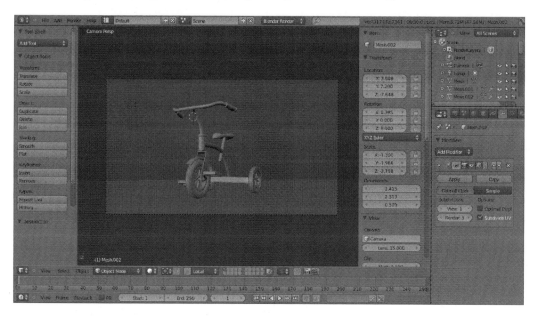

Setting up a 3-Point light rig

Earlier, we decided we wanted to use a 3-Point light rig. Let's review this quickly. A 3-Point light rig consists of three light sources:

- Key light
- Fill light
- Backlight

The **fill light** is placed to the side of the object, typically on the opposite side of the camera that the key light is on. Aimed toward the three-dimensional objects being illuminated, the purpose of the side light is to lighten some of the dark shadows and increase the perceived dimensionality of the three-dimensional object.

The backlight, or **rim light**, is important because its purpose is to create a sharp highlight on the edges of our three-dimensional object, forcing it to pop away from the background. This lamp is placed behind our object, opposite our camera. For best results, we should find a happy medium between the three-dimensional object and our camera to aim this lamp.

The **key light** is positioned next to the camera, that is, at the same distance from the three-dimensional grid and slightly to either side. In most cases, as in ours, the key light is aimed in the direction of the three-dimensional object, or objects, being lit.

Because the majority of the light that is used to light our tricycle will be coming from the sun, we can start constructing the 3-Point light rig with a sun lamp.

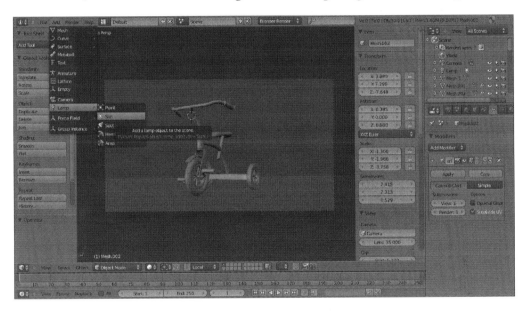

1. In Blender, add a Sun lamp by selecting **Add | Lamp | Sun**.

   ° Using either the *G-hotkey* or the Transform Widget, move the lamp so that it is just to the left of the camera.

   ° Rotate it using either the *R-hotkey* or the Rotation Widget, so that it's aimed in the direction of the tricycle.

    ° Give it a slight downward angle by rotating it along the horizontal axis (the local X axis). This will simulate the sun illuminating the tricycle from above.

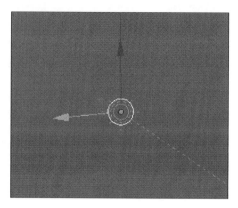

2. If you render it out (**Render | Render Image** or the *F12* key), you should get something similar to the following image:

 If you are a Macintosh user, you may have to press *fn + F12* to render the image properly. This bypasses the default Apple commands preprogrammed into the operating system.

Adjusting the lamp color

Remember that the sun lamp not only simulates the luminosity of the object, but the color as well. In order to change the various values associated with lamps in Blender, we need to take a look at the **Lamp** menu.

The Lamp menu

This menu button can be toggled between the **Lamp** menu and the **Material** menu, based on the type of object selected. If a lamp was selected, the **Lamp** menu would become active, and vice versa if a mesh was selected. Making sure our key light is selected, we can now access the **Lamp** menu.

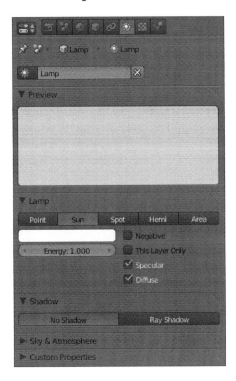

To better simulate light coming from the sun, we need to change the color that the key light produces to something comparable to natural sunlight. In our case, we can change the color to a slight yellow hue.

1. Click on the rounded rectangle found in the **Lamp** settings to bring up the color picker.

   ° Change the value to a slight yellow color—refer to the following image for guidance:

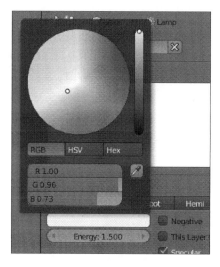

   ° When you're happy with the color selection, move the mouse off the color picker to close it:

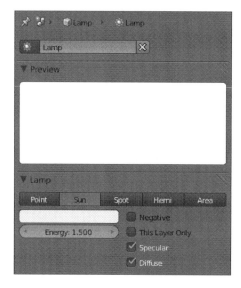

Adding shadows

Although our tricycle is in a three-dimensional medium, the render looks rather flat. This is partly due to a lack of shadows in our scene. Shadows have an amazing effect on a scene, as they can secure an object to the ground or push it up into the air. They can add another indicator of dimensionality to the three-dimensional object in the scene.

By default, Blender doesn't enable shadows. We have to explicitly tell the program to calculate them for our scene. Under the **Lamp** menu, there is a section for the **Shadow** settings, which is found directly underneath the **Lamp** settings we just adjusted.

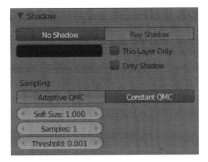

To enable shadows, you need to select the **Ray Shadow** radio button. This activates the shadow parameters, as we saw in the previous image. For now, leave these settings as they are, we'll play around with them later. Rendering out your scene now should result in something similar to the following image. If something doesn't seem right, go ahead and adjust some settings to fix it. When you're set, we can move on to add more lamps to our scene.

Adding a fill light

The next light to add is the fill light. In most cases, the fill light is found on the opposite side of the camera that the key light is on. In our case, we are going to use a Hemi lamp placed above the tricycle, simulating the light coming from the sky.

1. Add the Hemi lamp, and using either the *G-hotkey* or the Transform Widget, position the lamp above the tricycle by constraining it along the vertical z-axis.

Constraining along axes

There are two approaches to constraining a transformation along a particular axis. If you use the *G-hotkey*, you can constrain the object by pressing the *X* key, *Y* key, or *Z* key to constrain along the x, y, and z axes, respectively. To constrain using the Transform Widget, selecting one of the colored arrows will automatically constrain the transformation to that particular axis.

2. Change the color of the lamp to a sky blue and change the **Energy** to 0.5. This should result in an image similar to the following one:

Adding dimensionality with a backlight

The final light we need to add to complete our 3-Point light rig is the backlight, or rim light. The goal of this light is to add a strong highlight along the edges of our three-dimensional object, forcing it to pop away from the background.

1. Add another Sun lamp.

2. Position it using the *G-hotkey* or the Transform Widget so that the lamp is behind the triangle and opposite the camera.

3. Rotate it using the *R-hotkey* or the Rotation Widget so the light barely grazes the top of the tricycle (refer to the following image).

If we leave the rim light as is, it will wash out the shadow on our ground plane. To fix this, we need to move it to the first layer. With our rim light selected, enable the **This layer only** checkbox to tell it to only light the tricycle on the first layer.

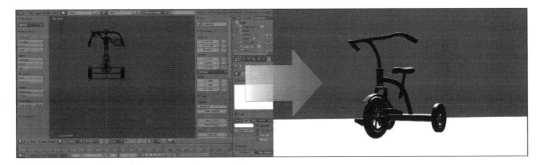

Good habits start early

The position of the Sun lamp has no effect on the way in which the image is rendered; Blender is only concerned with its angle. Why, then, are we moving the Sun lamps to these places in our scene? It may seem like extra work, but it serves more than a conceptual purpose. First, it gets us into the habit of moving our lamps around to where we imagine the source of light is coming from. Remember, some lamps do depend on the position of the lamp, such as the Spot lamp. Doing this habit with all the lamps puts us into the habit, so we don't confuse ourselves later.

Wrapping up

Continue to play around with the lamp settings and colors until you're satisfied with the result. Try new things and see what happens. It's surprising how many cool effects you find when you make a mistake.

Here is the final render we should have after lighting this scene. Once you have a result you're happy with, we can start adding materials and textures!

Summary

We've talked a lot about establishing and sticking to a workflow. This is very important when working professionally. An effective workflow can increase your productivity. We've also asked ourselves a lot of questions about our scene so that we can understand what's happening in our scene better. It's almost impossible to light a scene if we don't understand what's going on. These questions are aimed at guiding us and giving us a better understanding about where our scene is coming from, and it is at the moment we want to portray, and where it's going. If we can imagine that our scene has the potential to exist somewhere in the real world, then it will be a lot easier to produce a realistic result.

- What is the weather like?

- Where is the light coming from?

- What is the scale of these light sources in relation to our three-dimensional scene?

Using Blender's lamps, we were able to successfully simulate how our tricycle would look on a sunny, cloudless day. We also discussed:

- Applying a 3-Point light rig to our scene

- Adjusting the color of the lights to better reflect the sources they were intended to simulate

- Adding shadows to our scene to increase the credibility of the final render

- Using layers to better control the lighting in our scene

Now that we have a scene with a realistic light setup, we can move onto the next step—ambient occlusion!

3
Ambient Lighting Techniques in Blender

Ambient lighting is becoming an increasingly popular form of lighting in the computer graphics industry. Thanks to the hard work put in by the Blender developers, Blender v2.5 has three ambient lighting features, two of which have been added with the production of the Blender Institute's *Sintel* movie.

- Ambient occlusion
- Environment Lighting
- Indirect Lighting

The Blender Foundation, the organization behind Blender's development, introduced the concept of an "open movie" in 2005 with the production of *Elephants Dream*. It was a short animated film produced by the Foundation to test and improve Blender in a production environment. What makes the movie "open" is the fact that not only did the Foundation release the movie for everyone to watch, but they also released the production files as well. That means anyone can re-make these projects from the source files if they ever wanted to. Since then, the Blender Foundation created the Blender Institute, a studio dedicated to producing these open movies, which has gone on to create the short film *Big Buck Bunny*, the open game *Yo Frankie!*, and the currently in-production film, Sintel. The goal of each of these projects is to improve Blender in some way, shape, or form. For more information about these projects, visit the Blender Foundation's website at http://www.blender.org.

Blender uses two different algorithms to render ambient light—*raytraced* and *approximated*. The approximated method of rendering was introduced with the production of the Blender Institute's Big Buck Bunny.

Blender's raytraced ambient lighting algorithm is known to produce grainy render results and longer render times. It's also known to produce a *flickering* effect between frames in animations, an unwanted result addressed by the development team behind the Big Buck Bunny movie. To counter this effect, the team developed a new algorithm for ambient lighting—approximated ambient lighting. Because Blender only supported ambient occlusion at the time, it was the first feature to support the new algorithm. This new feature fixed many of the problems posed by the old algorithm, from requiring less time to computational power, but also producing a grain-free render.

Let's explore how we can implement these features into our own scene. We'll take a look at:

- How to activate the ambient occlusion, Environment Lighting, and Indirect Lighting settings

- How each feature affects our own scene

- How to customize each feature for a particular scene

- When to use one rendering algorithm over the other

Ambient occlusion

Ambient occlusion is a feature of 3D software used to simulate the effect of lighting refracting and reflecting off of objects in a scene. In a sense, it provides "even illumination" of objects, similar to the effect we were trying to simulate with our 3-Point light rig in the last chapter. In fact, ambient occlusion isn't a naturally occurring phenomenon—just a nice little 3D trick. When calculating ambient occlusion, Blender fires ambient light rays, which are occluded, or blocked, by objects in the 3D scene. When ambient light is occluded, it creates shadows and dark areas in the final render.

Raytraced ambient occlusion

The exact math behind ambient occlusion is rather difficult to understand, so for the sake of application-based situations, we'll just take a general look at how Blender approaches it. When ambient occlusion is turned on, Blender creates a hypothetical hemisphere around the objects in a 3D scene. Using the amount of light that is absorbed, or occluded, by the objects in the scene and how much is reflected back into the "sky" of the scene, Blender then calculates how the light will affect the mesh and its shadows.

Changing the options and settings

We can access Blender's ambient lighting features by looking at the **World** menu.

The following diagram shows Blender's **World** menu:

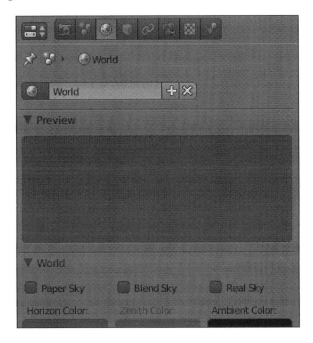

Although we can achieve a pretty good result without changing the default settings that Blender gives us for ambient occlusion, very rarely do those settings work in every situation. There are various settings and parameters we can set to fix that and achieve the effect we want. These options include: **Factor**, **Attenuation**, and **Sampling**.

The following image shows the raytraced **Ambient Occlusion** settings:

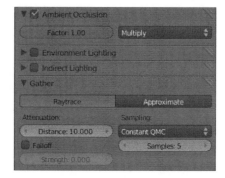

Factor

The Factor setting controls how much we want our ambient lighting technique to affect our scene. For example, a scene lit with an ambient occlusion factor of 0.3 will appear much darker than a scene lit with a factor of 0.8.

In the following image, the scene on the left has a Factor value of 0.3, while the scene on the right has a Factor value of 0.8

Take note that in order for ambient occlusion to work properly in our lamp-less scene, we need to change the blend setting from Multiply to Add—this is the setting next to the Factor value. If we don't do this, the render will appear black. This is because Blender renders the scene and then combines the result with the ambient occlusion pass. But because the Multiply algorithm results favors black as the dominant color, ambient occlusion seems to have no effect at all due to the fact that there are no lights in the scene.

With a Factor value of 1.0, in the following image, the scene on the left is rendered with **Multiply** enabled, while the scene on the right is rendered with **Add** enabled:

Sampling

Sampling refers to settings that control the quality of the ambient occlusion, including the number of samples and the sampling algorithm.

Samples control the number of rays that Blender uses to calculate the effect the ambient occlusion algorithm will have on our scene—the higher this number is, the better our final result will be. There is a downside, though—as the number of samples increases, so does the time it takes for Blender to render the scene. Because the number of samples controls the precision and the quality of the result of the algorithm, this would make sense—it would take a computer more time to do more work. There are three raytracing algorithms available for Blender:

- Constant QMC
- Adaptive QMC
- Constant jittered

We don't need to concern ourselves with the differences between these algorithms—Constant QMC is the default algorithm and usually gives the best quality in most situations. If you're interested in learning more about the specifics about QMC sampling, visit http://www.blender.org/development/release-logs/blender-246/qmc-sampling/.

Attenuation

Attenuation deals with distance and falloff. The distance parameter controls the length of the rays Blender uses in occlusion calculation. If the falloff setting is activated, it controls the amount of energy falloff these rays have. It's similar to the falloff factor of Blender's lamps—this setting determines how much energy is lost as you distance yourself from the source of the lamp. The Strength setting serves as a multiplier for the Distance value, meaning the higher the Strength value is, the shorter shadows will look in the final render.

With a Factor value of 1.0 in the following image, the scene on the left has Falloff disabled, while the scene on the right has Falloff enabled with a Strength value of 2:

 What happened to the Influence settings?

The **Influence** settings, similar to the **Blending** settings found in previous versions of Blender, have been removed in Blender v2.5 and replaced with two blending options: **Multiply** and **Add**.

Energy and color

Just as you can set and adjust the intensity and color of Blender's lamps, you can set and adjust the intensity and color of the occlusion as well. More often than not, the default **Energy** setting is more than enough. The color will always vary based on the scene.

Approximate ambient occlusion

Although raytraced ambient occlusion will produce good results with the proper settings, when it comes to incorporating ambient occlusion with an animation, there are still some problems. Most notably, the grainy images produced by the raytraced ambient occlusion algorithm result in a flickering effect as the animation moves from frame to frame. The render time had to be addressed as well—because raytraced ambient occlusion is so computationally expensive, it wouldn't make sense to use it in an animation.

A new approach to ambient occlusion

The team behind the Blender Institute's *Big Buck Bunny* movie decided that in order to solve these problems, they needed to approach ambient occlusion from a different angle all-together. The resulting work they did over the duration of the project introduced this new approach, which is known as *approximate ambient occlusion*.

This method isn't ideal for every situation, such as raytraced ambient occlusion, and it may require some tweaking to get it right. The results, though, are both grain-free and require less time to render, fixing some of the problems posed by the raytracing algorithm.

Like all new technology, the new algorithm wasn't perfect and posed some problems of its own. One of the biggest problems the team ran into was that this new method resulted in too much occlusion when two faces behind one another faced in the same direction.

In the following image, geometry on the interior of the rabbit hole is over-occluded, a downfall of the approximated algorithm:

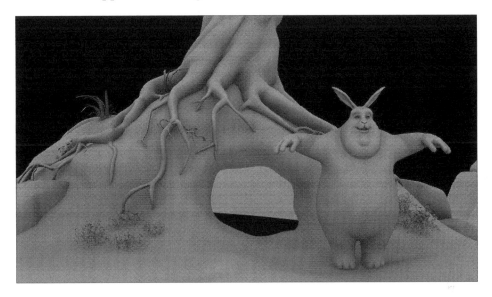

New algorithm, new settings

When we first take a look at the settings that control approximate ambient occlusion, we see a completely different set of options to choose from. Although they're grouped under the same sections as raytraced ambient occlusion (**Sampling, Attenuation**, and **Influence**), the settings used to control these aspects of ambient occlusion differ slightly.

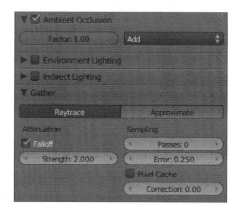

Sampling

Approximated ambient occlusion introduces four new settings to deal with image sampling:

* Passes
* Error
* Pixel cache
* Correction

Passes controls the number of preprocessing passes the computer will make before rendering to reduce the potential for over-occlusion. **Error** represents the error tolerance—lower values will produce better results, because there isn't much room for miscalculation. Unsurprisingly, the lower the **Error** value, the longer it takes to render the image.

Attenuation and influence

Attenuation, in this case, is only concerned with the falloff factor of the ambient occlusion. When enabled, the rays of light used to determine ambient occlusion are affected by this falloff factor, which is taken into account when rendering. Blender treats the falloff factor of ambient occlusion similarly to the falloff setting included with its lamps—as an object moves farther away from the light source, the effect the light will have on the object decreases.

Advantages and disadvantages

Both of these algorithms approach ambient occlusion from different angles, each with their own advantages and disadvantages. Let's take another look at these differences.

Raytraced ambient occlusion

The advantages of raytraced ambient occlusion are as follows:

- Realistic/physically accurate results
- Great for still images

The disadvantages are:

- Images contain some degree of noise
- Flickering occurs between frames in animation
- Longer render times
- More stress on the computer's CPU

Approximated ambient occlusion

The advantages of approximated ambient occlusion are:

- Faster render times
- Less computing power needed
- Noise-free
- Good for both still images and animation

The disadvantages are:

- When faces behind one another are facing the same direction, it results in over-occlusion
- A bit harder to configure for more complex scenes

Environment Lighting

Environment Lighting is a new feature introduced with the Blender v2.5 lineup. The algorithm uses light from the environment to light the scene in addition to any lights we may have.

In addition to the Energy value, which controls how much environment light Blender will take into account, there are three sources we can tell Blender to look at for light information. They are:

- White
- Sky color
- Sky texture

White, of course, tells Blender to assume that all environment light has a white color. This will result in a render remarkably similar to a scene rendered with ambient occlusion.

The following scene illustrates a raytraced Environment Lighting with an Energy value of 1.0:

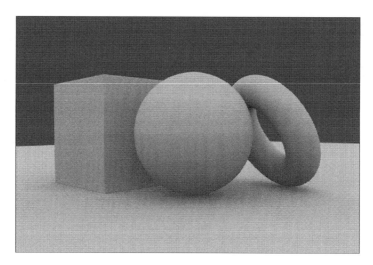

- We can also use Blender's World values to define the color of the environment light by changing the Sky color or adding a Sky texture.

Note that the term "Sky" refers to Blender's digital sky, or the area around our scene. This doesn't necessarily mean the area above our objects, like the real sky.

To change the color of the Sky, we need to manipulate the **Horizon Color** value, found under the **World** settings in Blender's **World** menu.

For example, if we change the Horizon's color to a blue hue, we will get a render with a blue tone to it. This is because when we have the environment light source set to Sky color, Blender renders our Environment Lighting under the assumption that all ambient light has the color of the Sky.

The following image shows an image rendered with the Sky color value of R: 0.52, G: 0.75, B: 1.0, and an Energy value of 5.0:

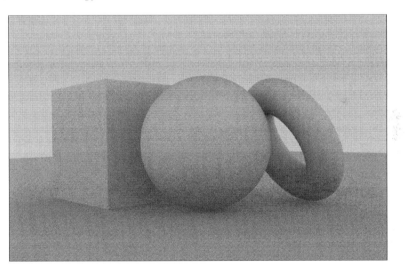

- The final source Blender can get light information from is the Sky texture, which is especially useful when using HDR lighting. **HDR** stands for **High Dynamic Range**, and it is used to refer to images that contain a high range of color—that is, more than a typical JPEG or PNG image would hold. HDR lighting is a common lighting technique in the computer graphics industry, giving artists an easy way to fake realistic lighting conditions.

Lighting a scene with HDR lighting

- Let's take a look at how we can light a scene with a High Dynamic Range image. For simplicity, download the blend and texture files named `hdri.blend` and `hdri_example.png`, respectively, from `http://www.cgshark.com/lighting-and-rendering/`. This scene has been pre-built with some materials and textures included, so all we have to do is set up the lighting.

- The following screenshot shows the file `hdri.blend` when first opened:

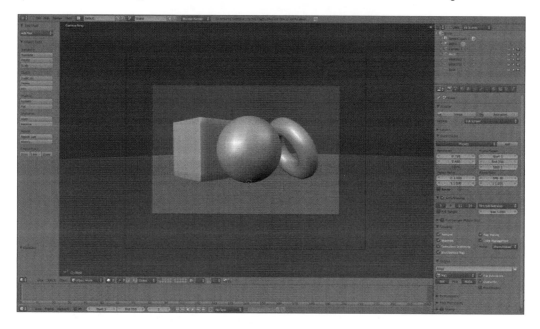

To create a Sky texture, make sure we start in the **World** menu. Blender v2.5 associates the **Texture** menu with the menu previously used—for example, if you were editing a material, switching over to the **Texture** menu from the Material menu would associate that texture with the selected material. We'll discuss this in greater detail later.

From the **World** menu, select the **Texture** menu icon. You should see a list of features similar to the screenshot below:

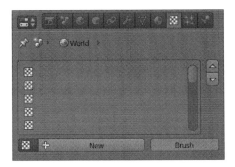

The preceding screenshot shows Blender's **Texture** menu.

To add the image we're going to use to light our scene, we need to add a new texture—to do this, click the **New** button in the **Texture** menu. This will present us with an entirely new array of options to choose from.

Blender's default textures settings window looks like the following screenshot:

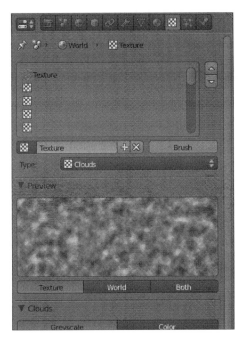

- We first need to tell Blender to look for an image to use as a texture—to do this, we need to change the texture Type. Blender supports numerous types of textures, but we will take a deeper look at those options later. For now, we just need to select the **Image or Movie** option.

- This will once again present us with more settings, this time, specific to the **Image or Movie** texture type. Although Blender now knows to look for an image, it still doesn't know where to look. We still need to tell Blender what image to use. To do this:

  1. Click on the **New** button under the **Image** settings.

  2. Set the source type to **File**.

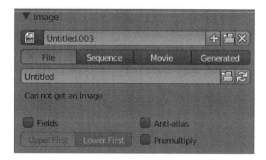

  3. Under the source type buttons, there's a file path text area with the word **Untitled** in it. Select the folder icon next to this text area and navigate to the image file that we downloaded earlier—environment.png.

4. Under the **Mapping** settings—farther down in the menu—set the **Texture Coordinates** value from **View** to **AngMap**, as shown in the following screenshot:

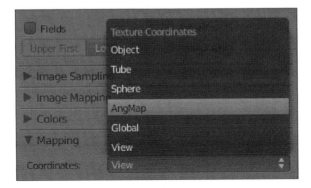

5. Under the **Influence** settings, deselect the **Blend** option and instead, select the **Horizon** option, as shown in the following screenshot:

6. Now go back to the **World** menu and activate the **Environment Lighting** settings. This is where we tell Blender to light our scene using our Sky image.

7. Set the **Energy** value to 3.0, and set the **light source** option to **Sky Texture**.

If we render out our image, we get something similar to the image below.

The following image shows a raytraced Environment Lighting with an Energy value of 3.0 and source set to the Sky texture:

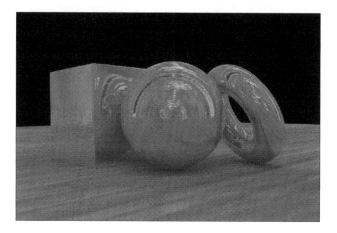

 Note that our Sky value is set to **Premultiplied** in the render settings. This renders the background as an alpha value, instead of the Sky texture we created. This makes our render a little easier on the eyes.

Indirect Lighting

Like Environment Lighting, Indirect Lighting was added with the release of Blender v2.5. This algorithm works in a similar fashion to the Environment Lighting algorithm, except that instead of taking light directly from the environment, Blender bounces light off of objects in our scene and uses the reflected light to illuminate our objects.

The following image shows the default Indirect Lighting settings:

This is most useful when using a mesh to illuminate a scene, instead of a lamp. Unfortunately, this algorithm also still has some issues—for example, it only renders a mesh as a lamp if we use the approximate algorithm and not the raytraced algorithm.

The following image shows a Mesh light rendered with the Approximate Indirect Lighting algorithm:

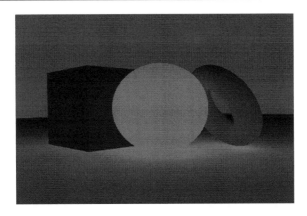

Applying ambient lighting to our working scene

Now that we know which algorithm to use, let's open up our original scene, `outdoor.blend`, and turn on ambient lighting there.

If you have renamed your scene since the beginning of *Chapter 2, Outdoor Lighting: Setting Up Our Scene*, make sure you open the file that contains your working scene, including the light rig and tricycle.

Navigate to the **World** menu and turn on **Ambient Occlusion**. The only setting we are going to change is the algorithm to use—the default, which Blender provides, is raytraced ambient occlusion. We want a noise-free render, so we are going to use approximated ambient occlusion instead. Select the **Approximate** button at the top of the menu box to switch algorithms.

Finishing up

We're done! We've successfully added ambient occlusion to our scene. Render out your image now, and you'll see something similar to the following image:

Summary

We've covered a lot about ambient occlusion, discussing not only the theory and settings behind it, but also how to apply it to our scene. We've looked at:

- How Blender treats ambient lighting
- The different algorithms for rendering ambient lighting, including raytraced and approximate ambient lighting
- The differences between ambient occlusion, environment lighting, and indirect lighting
- How to use each algorithm in a practical setting
- How ambient occlusion affects our own scene
- How to apply it to our working file

Now it's on to one of the more fun parts of lighting and rendering—creating and editing textures and materials!

4

Outdoor Scene: Adding Materials

Now that we've lit our scene properly, we can begin to take a look at the next step of the process—adding and editing materials. Materials in Blender are what give meshes a particular look or "feel". This includes:

- Color
- Texture
- Shading
- Reflections

We are going to take a look at these as well as some other properties associated with materials and textures in Blender. In this chapter, we will:

- Look at how Blender deals with materials
- How to create and edit material properties
- Various algorithms Blender uses to render materials
- How to create semi-transparent and reflective objects
- How to create materials specific to our tricycle scene

Creating a new material

There used to be multiple approaches to creating a new material in earlier versions of Blender, but in v2.5, the process has been reduced to one menu to eliminate any confusion or unnecessary use of interface space.

Remember when we learned that the menu buttons for the **Lights** menu and the **Material** menu are toggled depending on whether a light or a mesh is selected in our 3D scene? We are going to take a look at the **Material** menu this time—if you select any mesh in the scene, you should see that the **Material** menu becomes accessible.

Taking a closer look at the Materials menu

Before we can effectively create materials in Blender, we need to understand what settings control what aspect of rendering and why we should use each. Otherwise, there wouldn't be much point in randomly selecting buttons, hoping that eventually one of them will work. When we see the **Material** menu for the first time, we see a blank materials list and a material add/selection button.

The **Material** menu, at an initial glance, looks like the following screenshot:

Go ahead and press **New** because we don't have any materials in our scene yet. We need to create one to take a look at the options available. Once we've created a material, our menu changes to look something similar to the following screenshot:

The **Material** menu looks like the following screenshot after a new material is created:

Now we have a number of settings available to us that we can use to customize our material. These settings include:

- Material name and type
- Preview
- Diffuse and specular
- Shading
- Transparency and mirror
- Subsurface scattering

Material name, type, and preview

In order to keep our materials organized in our 3D scene, we can give each a unique name that describes what the material is. By default, Blender named our material `Material`. Not very unique or interesting is it? Go ahead and change it to `test_material`—no, it may not be much more intuitive, but it better explains the purpose of our material, which is the goal.

Blender provides us with four available material types—two of which are new additions as of Blender v2.5:

- Surface
- Wire
- Volume
- Halo

The **Surface** mesh window looks like the following screenshot:

Surface is the default material type. It's a typical 3D surface mesh, just like you would find in any 3D program. Most often, this is the type that we will use in our 3D scenes, because it most effectively resembles the surface of most objects in the real world.

The following image is the peanut character we looked at when discussing light rigs rendered with white material set to Surface type:

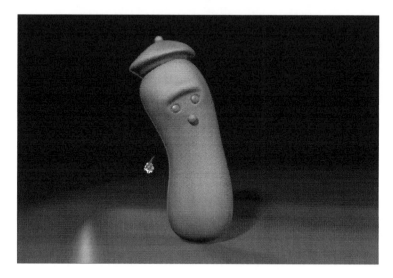

Wire renders our mesh as a wireframe model, instead of a solid polygonal model like the **Surface** material type does.

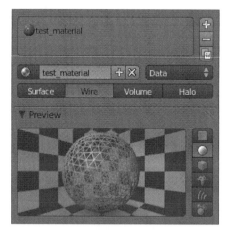

Rendering in *wireframe* is useful to showcase how an object's mesh is laid out for a portfolio—a clean mesh is a good mesh.

The following image is rendered with white material set to **Wire** type:

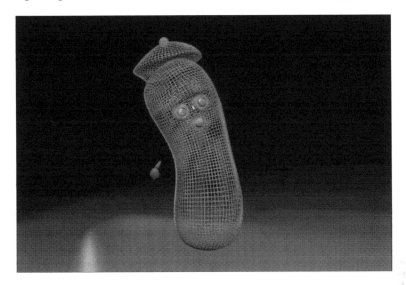

The next available material type in Blender is a new addition—**Volume**. This is an attempt at creating volume primitives to compete with those of programs such as Autodesk Maya. Although still at an early stage, this material type can prove very useful in the right situations.

When this type is selected, Blender uses the mesh as a cage, and creates a volumetric fog effect within the parameters of this cage. This effect is well achieved in the following image, which is rendered with white material set to **Volume** type:

The final material type found in Blender is not new—the **Halo** material type has been around nearly as long as Blender has. This material is extremely useful in creating a *glowing* effect.

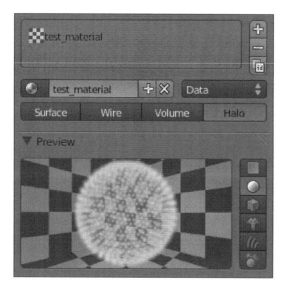

Although the default settings aren't great and it takes some major tweaking to get reasonable results, the **Halo** material type is used often and can prove worth the effort. The following is an image rendered with white material set to Halo type:

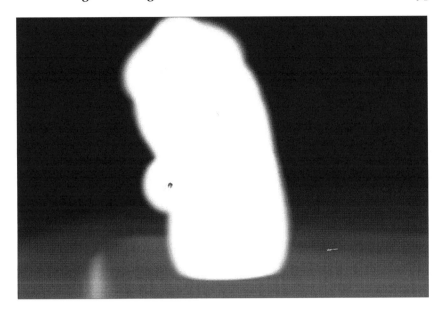

Preview

Notice how the image under **Preview** changed as we looked at the different material types—this is because the **Preview** image updates itself automatically to simulate what the selected material would look like on various meshes, including:

- A flat plane
- A sphere (which is the default preview mesh)
- A cube
- A *Suzanne* mesh
- Particle strands
- Environment-mapped sphere

> Suzanne is an inside joke of the Blender community. During development of one of the early versions of Blender, one of the developers modeled a monkey head and included it in the primitive object options alongside the usual cube, plane, sphere, and so on. The monkey head has since been dubbed "Suzanne" and has been included in every Blender release since.

We may choose to use a different preview mesh depending on how our materials are mapped onto our objects. We'll take a close look at when to use each mesh when we talk more about textures.

Diffuse and specular

Every object in the real world has diffuse and specular properties. The term **diffuse** refers to the overall color produced when light is reflected, refracted, and absorbed by an object. **Specular** simply refers to the highlights of an object—metallic and plastic materials tend to have higher and harder specular properties than something like cardboard or a woolen blanket. These highlights are really more of a 3D trick that actual "highlights". More often than not, highlights in a real photograph are the result of the light coming directly from a light source, such as a window or light bulb, and bouncing straight into the viewer's eye. The specular value controls how that effect is supposed to behave in our render.

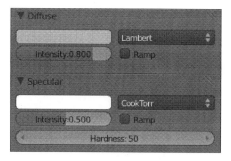

Take this clock for example—as we can see, there is a very high specular highlight. This is why the highlight on the black plastic border is so sharp. If this clock were to have a lower specular value, the highlight would neither be as sharp, nor as prominent.

Diffuse shader models

Blender supports numerous algorithms that we can use to render diffuse materials. Each can be used to create a different effect, from the most abstract to the hyper-realistic. These models include:

- Lambert
- Oren-Nayar
- Toon
- Minnaert
- Fresnel

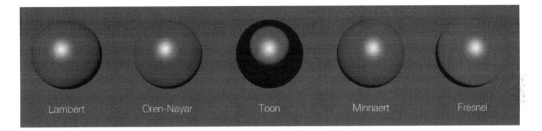

We are only going to concern ourselves with the "Lambert" shading model, because it's one of the most versatile algorithms that Blender provides and can be applied to almost any situation. If you're interested in learning more about how the other shaders work and why Blender includes them, feel free to visit `http://wiki.blender.org/index.php/Doc:Manual/Materials/Properties/Diffuse_Shaders`.

Specular shader models

In the same way diffuse shader models calculate how the diffuse color will appear on a material, specular shader models control how the specular color, or highlight, of a material will look.

These models include:

- CookTorr
- Phong
- Blinn
- Toon
- WardIso

Experiment with each of these and see what results you get—we will focus primarily with **Blinn** and **Phong** specular highlights.

Shading

The **Shading** settings deal directly with how light interacts with our material. **Emit** dictates how much "light" the material gives off. In computer graphics, it's common to only take into account the effect direct light has on an object, and unless we use ambient lighting, Blender won't take any indirect light into account. With the Emit parameter, we can use meshes in our scene as lights as well, and because Blender needs ambient lighting to render this light, we get the added value of indirect lighting as well. **Ambient** determines how heavily the material is affected by light from the surrounding environment. **Translucency** tells Blender how much light can pass through the material.

There are also three checkboxes that we can activate if we choose:

- Shadeless
- Tangent Shading
- Cubic Interpolation

Shadeless, as we can guess, tells Blender to throw away everything else we tell it about the color of our material and render the object with a single color value. This flattens out the object immediately, leaving the outline to be the only discernable part of the render.

Tangent Shading considers the direction of the surface tangents when rendering—it typically results in an anisotropic highlight. **Cubic Interpolation** tells Blender to use a cubic algorithm when rendering an image, compared to the default linear algorithm.

Transparency and mirror

Transparency and mirror are extremely useful when working with glass and metal materials. Both features have numerous parameters that we can use to adjust how we want our material to look.

Configuring the transparency settings

To enable transparency for a material, select the checkbox next to the **Transparency** menu heading. Blender approaches transparency in two ways:

- Z Transparency
- Raytrace

Z Transparency uses something called an alpha buffer to calculate the transparency of an object. Blender calculates this type of transparency by mixing colors of objects overlapping each other. For example, if a semi-transparent red sphere was placed in front of a yellow one, we would see the intersecting section take on an orange hue.

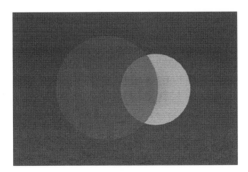

This algorithm isn't by any means physically accurate and doesn't require much computing power to create. Because of the amount of tweaking it would take to get right, we are only going to work with **raytraced transparency**. Like other raytraced features in Blender, raytraced transparency is mathematically calculated and physically accurate, requiring more computational power and longer render times.

To enable raytraced transparency, select the **Raytrace** button at the top
of the **Transparency** settings.

We immediately see a long list of settings we can configure—let's take a quick look at
each of them.

- IOR (Index of Refraction)
- Filter
- Falloff
- Limit
- Depth
- Gloss

IOR, or Index of Refraction, is one of the most important settings we will deal with
when working with transparency. Everything in the real world that has some degree
of transparency has an index of refraction. This is simply a number that dictates how
far light is refracted when it passes through the object, resulting in the distortion of
objects behind it. Take a look at the image of the shot glass below—notice how the
pattern is warped when you look through the glass.

Jenny Downing   http://www.flickr.com/photos/jenny-pics/2872292856/

Filter controls how much of the material's diffuse color is blended with the material's transparency. This simulates light absorption in materials like glass.

With an Index of Refraction of 1.55 (the IOR of consumer-grade glass), the image on the left is rendered with a Filter value of 0, while the image on the right is rendered with a Filter value of 0.5.

Falloff deals with the Filter setting, telling Blender how much blending to actually do between the material color and the transparency values. By default, Blender uses a Falloff value of 1.0, which means that the light rays lose power at a linear, constant rate. The effect this value has on the image is so subtle that unless it interacts with another parameter in the scene in a specific, user-defined way, there's no real need to change it.

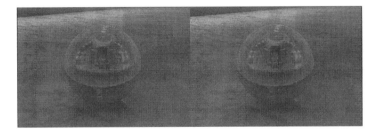

With a Filter value of 0.5, the image on the left is rendered with a Falloff value of 1.0, while the image on the right is rendered with a Filter value of 0.1.

Limit sets the maximum distance that light can travel through a transparent material before being completely filtered. A value of 0 disables this feature.

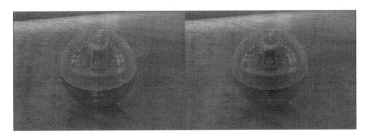

With a Filter value of 0.5, the image on the left is rendered with a Limit value of 0, while the image on the right is rendered with a Limit value of 3.0.

Depth deals with the number of acceptable inter-refractions calculated—a higher value here will result in a higher resolution transparency effect. For good results at a reasonable render time, a **Depth** value of 6 works well, but this can range anywhere between 1 and 10, which is shown below. Note how the lower **Depth** value creates a dark shadow in the middle of our transparent object—this is due to the lack of reflection resolution and can be eliminated with a higher **Depth** value.

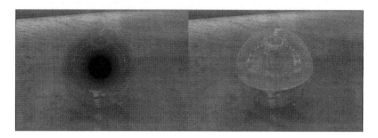

The last aspect of transparency that we need to look at is the **Gloss** settings. **Gloss** allows us to render fuzzy refractions and reflections, which is extremely useful when rendering materials like frosted glass. It's a bit sensitive though—many times, reducing the **Amount** value to 0.95 is more than enough (1.0 renders no gloss effect).

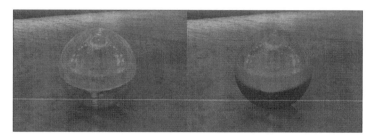

The image on the left is rendered with a Gloss value of 1.0, while the image on the right is rendered with a Gloss setting of 0.8.

Configuring mirror settings

The **Mirror** menu, like the **Transparency** menu, has an array of settings we can use to customize our reflections. Unlike the **Transparency** feature, though, reflections in Blender are purely raytraced—unless, of course, we use a texture map on the material's reflection channel, but that's something completely different all together. Under the **Mirror** menu, we can use the following parameters to change the appearance of our reflections:

- Reflectivity
- Max Dist.
- Depth
- Fresnel
- Gloss

These settings all act the same way as their corresponding settings in the **Transparency** menu, but they affect the reflections instead of the transparency. The following image is rendered with a Reflectivity value of 0.6 and a Fresnel value of 2.0:

Creating materials for our scene

Let's create our first material for our tricycle—the red paint. Begin by opening our scene, `outdoor.blend`, and select any part of the tricycle body. To make our jobs easier, the various parts on our tricycle have been pre-named, so we won't have too much trouble figuring out which meshes need which materials.

 If you renamed your `outdoor.blend` file, make sure you are opening the one that we lit together earlier.

1. Select any part of the tricycle body (`bike_support`, for example) by right-clicking on the mesh within the 3D view or by selecting the name in the Outliner.

2. Add a new material (refer to *Creating a new material* section), renaming it to `red_metal`.

We want a red metal material—let's start by changing the color. Using the color picker found under the **Diffuse** settings, change the color of our newly created material to a red hue. The settings I used are found below:

The next step is to change the *hardness* of the material. This will tell Blender how sharp the specular highlight will appear. Under the **Specular** settings, go ahead and bump this up to 200.

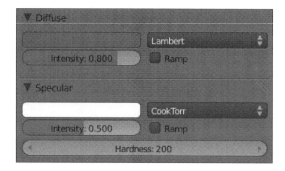

This brings us to our next step. Very rarely in real life do we find materials with a pure white specular highlight. In our case, the red paint will most likely produce an off-white, pink-ish highlight. Using the color picker underneath the **Specular** settings, change the color to a light pink. Also, make sure to change the specular shading model to Blinn (refer to the *Specular shader models* section earlier in the chapter).

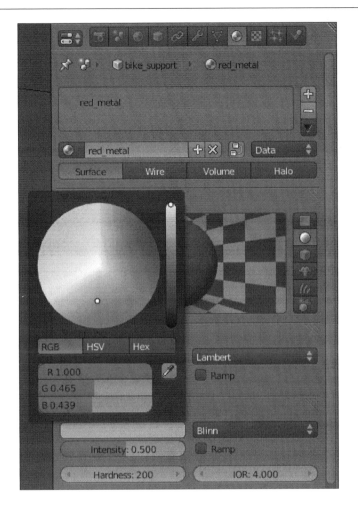

Now we can add reflections, which really add to the believability of our render. Turn on the **Mirror** settings by selecting the checkbox next to the **Mirror** heading.

1. Turn up the **Reflectivity** setting to 0.05—we don't want the reflections to overpower the render, but we do want there to be a hint of their existence.

2. Change the **Depth** setting to 6. This will increase the resolution quality of the reflections themselves.

3. Finally, change the **Gloss** amount to 0.95. Nothing in nature—with the exception of a mirror has perfect reflectivity. To be honest, even mirrors have defects. This will *blur* our reflections so that they don't appear as crisp.

4. Add our newly created material to the rest of the tricycle's body (`front_support`, `bike_support`, `seat_support`, and `bike_base`).

5. Render out our image and we should get something similar to the image below:

Let's burn some rubber!

The next material we are going to create is the rubber material for our tires. This is a nice contrast to the metal material we just created in that we are aiming to replicate a soft, diffuse rubber material, compared to a hard, highly specular metal material. Select the front wheel and let's begin!

1. Create a new material () and name it `tire`.

2. Using the color picker underneath the **Diffuse** settings, change the material color to a dark gray.

 Why not black? Just like nothing in real life is pure white, nothing in real life is pure black, either. An off-black is a more realistic representation of what "black" might look like in the real world.

The key to creating realistic specular highlights on materials really comes down to color. Metals and other materials with really sharp specular highlights typically have really bright speculars, like the red metal we created earlier. Really soft materials, on the other hand, have a softer specular highlight with a color much closer to the diffuse color of the material. This is how we are going to approach the specular highlight on our tire material.

1. Change the specular color to a medium gray hue and turn down the hardness to 10. This really spreads the specular out across the mesh, creating a much softer effect.

2. The default specular shading model (**CookTorr**) works just fine for our needs. Unless you're interested in experimenting a bit, there isn't a need to change it.

We now need to apply this new material to the rest of the tricycle's tires—this includes the following meshes:

- `left_wheel_tire`
- `right_wheel_tire`
- `front_wheel_tire`

Taking a shortcut

When working in a production setting, learning when to take shortcuts is essential to returning a product on time. In our case, we are going to take a little shortcut of our own to simplify the creation of our next material—the gray metal that we will use on a lot of the remaining features of our tricycle.

Duplicating a material

The first thing we want to do is duplicate the `red_metal` texture we created earlier. In Blender terms, we are creating a **single-user copy**. To do this, select the handlebar mesh (`handle_bar`) and add the red metal material. Notice the number next to the material name—this tells us how many objects in our 3D scene are currently using that material.

To create a single-user copy, click on this number and rename our new material to `grey_metal`.

1. Change the diffuse color of our newly duplicated material to a medium gray, using the color picker underneath the **Diffuse** settings.

2. Because we changed the diffuse color, we need to change the specular color as well. Under the **Specular** settings, change the specular color to an off-white.

3. Apply our new material to the following meshes:

   ◦ handle_bar

   ◦ front_tire_support

   ◦ left_pedal_bar

   ◦ right_pedal_bar

   ◦ front_wheel_rim

   ◦ left_wheel_rim

   ◦ right_wheel_rim

Almost done!

We have two more simple materials to create for our tricycle—a red plastic and a white plastic.

1. Select a pedal. Create a new material and, using the color picker, change the diffuse color to the same red we used for the red metal material. Rename the material to red_plastic.

2. Now the only thing we need to change is the specular highlight—all of the other settings are fine as they are. Change the specular color to a slightly lighter red than the diffuse color.

3. Now select the seat of the tricycle and add our new plastic material. Duplicate it and rename it to white_plastic.

4. Change the diffuse color to an off-white. Because nothing in the real world is truly white, we can even add a slight hint of yellow to make the material a little more believable.

5. Once again, change the specular color to almost a pure white.

6. Add the white plastic material to both handlebar grips, the seat, the spokes in-between the three wheels, and the plastic cover above the front wheel.

7. Now we can render out our image to see how we're doing!

Changing the environment

Our tricycle is complete, but the environment it's in certainly isn't. Remember we decided to not explicitly render our ground plane—let's tackle that first.

We want to tell Blender that the ground plane will only receive shadows. Luckily for us, there's a setting for that.

1. With our ground plane selected, add a new material and name it ground_plane.

2. At the very bottom of the material settings list, under the **Shadow** settings, select **Shadows Only**. This tells Blender to only receive shadows on the mesh, but not to render the mesh itself.

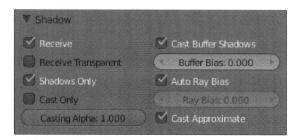

3. That's it! Now our render will leave out the ground plane, leaving the shadows untouched.

Finishing up

The last thing to take care of is the image background. Right now, it's rather bland. To fix this, we are going to add a gradient to our background using the **World** settings.

Under the **World** menu, there's a section of settings called **World**. This controls the background of the render. Select the **Blend Sky** option — this tells Blender to create a gradient between the **Horizon Color** and the **Zenith Color**. For our intents and purposes, we only need to change the **Zenith Color** to a light gray color. Now if we render our final image, we should see something similar to the following image:

Let's review!

Congratulations! We've successfully lit our first scene! We've also learned a lot during the process, so let's take some time and review it. Throughout the course of this project, we've looked at:

- Establishing a workflow
- Questions we should ask ourselves before lighting a scene
- How to add and edit lamps in Blender and how to effectively set up a 3-Point light rig, based on our object's environment
- How ambient occlusion works and how we can best apply it to our scene
- How to add and edit materials and textures in Blender

Reviewing our workflow

The importance of developing a good, efficient workflow cannot be stressed enough. Once we have a workflow in place, our projects become much more productive and we'll find we can get more done much faster. As every artist is different, there isn't a workflow that works for everyone. Earlier, we took a look at a workflow that made sense for our project. This included:

- Evaluating our scene
- Planning how to lay out the lamps in our scene
- Creating and setting the lamps, intensities, colors, and so on
- Adding materials and textures
- Tweaking!

Evaluating the scene

Before we can even start lighting, we need to completely understand our scene, not only in respect to where it's coming from, but in respect to where it's going as well. We need to ask ourselves questions and convince ourselves that this environment has the possibility of existence—otherwise, we won't be able to create a realistic sense of lighting.

Remember to ask the right questions

Before we lit our scene, we learned that it helps to ask ourselves questions about where our scene is coming from, where it is at the moment we want to capture, and where it's going after that moment; this doesn't necessarily mean where our scene is literally going—it may not be going anywhere in that sense. We should be asking ourselves questions about the weather, current lighting conditions, the direction and source of the light, and so on. All of these questions should be geared toward getting us focused on what's going on in our scene.

Planning our lamp setup

After we've convinced ourselves that our scene could exist somewhere in the real world, we can start thinking about how we want to simulate the effect we want. This includes choosing which light rig to use and how to set it up.

Remember to think about how light would react in a physical environment—this can help you simulate how it will look in our 3D scene as well.

Actually setting up our lamps

With our lamp layout in mind, we can now create, position, and edit the lamps we want in our scene. We can also choose to set things such as light intensity, color, shadow, and so on. This is more time consuming than anything—if we had properly planned out our lamps before, we shouldn't have too much of a hard time getting them to render correctly.

Remember that there are numerous lamp types in Blender:

- Point lamp
- Sun lamp
- Spot lamp
- Hemi lamp
- Area lamp

It's important to know what unique properties each of these lamp types possess and why we should use one over the other. To add any of these to our scene, we can simply look under the **Add** menu: **Add | Lamp | [Lamp Type]**. Also remember that the **Lights** menu and the **Materials** menu is toggled depending on the type of object we have selected—if we forget this, we might get really confused really fast. Luckily, Blender draws lamps in the 3D viewport in a very distinct way, and it is easy to change a lamp's type right on the spot, so we can clearly distinguish what object is what in our scene.

Under the **Lights** menu, we learned that we can change settings such as intensity, color, and shadow values to create a more realistic, or believable, render. If you haven't played with any settings, try some out now. We've already successfully completed the first project, so it won't hurt to test some things out! The worst thing that can happen is you produce a crummy render, but who hasn't at one point or another? Don't be afraid of failure—you may learn something you didn't know before!

Reviewing light rigs

We learned that light rigs are systems of lights structured in a way that successfully lights an object, or objects, in our scene. In our particular case, we used a 3-Point light rig, which consisted of three components:

- A key light
- A fill light
- A rim light (or backlight)

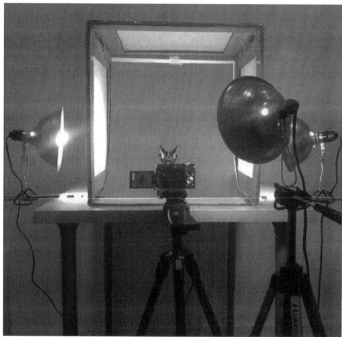

Kirby Kerr http://www.flickr.com/photos/rotofugi/3863563133/sizes/o/

The image we just saw is an example of a 3-Point light rig in a photography studio. The light on the left and right serve as fill lights, while the light directly behind the camera is the key light. This setup would be used to photograph a product such as a toy or an electronic device.

In case we all forgot, the key light is the main light used to light our scene. Many times in lighting conditions such as product presentations (like our own project and the one in the image above), the key light is located directly next to the camera. The fill light is set at a slightly lower intensity than the key light on the opposite side of the camera and to the side of the objects in our scene. Finally, the rim light is placed behind the object, typically with a really high intensity value, facing the camera. This creates a *rim* highlight, forcing the scene to *pop* from the background.

Of course, we can use any number of lights to achieve the effect we want—many times, scenes require more than one light rig in conjunction with linking lights with specific layers to get it right.

Adding materials

Our lights are done, but our scene still looks…bland. To really make our render look amazing, we can add materials. Have fun with this and really think about the different properties of each of the objects in our scene—we'll take a look at how to create unique textures in GIMP and how we can bring them into Blender in our next project to help with this as well.

Ambient lighting

Light, as we learned, is reflected and refracted until all light is absorbed. This leads to colors mixing with each other in our scene. In computer graphics, this effect is known as **Global illumination** or **GI**. Global illumination is another term for ambient lighting.

With the new release of Blender v2.5, we have a whole new set of ambient lighting techniques and options to use in our scene, including ambient occlusion and environment lighting. Blender uses two different rendering algorithms with these features:

- Raytraced ambient lighting
- Approximated ambient lighting

We learned that **Raytraced Ambient Occlusion** relies heavily on mathematical compuations to render properly, which, unfortunately, leads to longer render times. It also produces a certain amount of noise, which causes animations to "flicker" when played. To fix this, Blender introduced the second algorithm we looked at, which is now known as **Approximated Ambient Occlusion**. This not only fixed the flickering problem with animations (images rendered with this algorithm are noise-free), it also required less computing power and less time to render. Remember, though, that this new algorithm also produced too much occlusion when faces behind one another are facing the same direction.

Blender material basics

This is one of the biggest changes to Blender's interface that we've looked at so far. Although the underlying approaches to materials is the same as it was in previous versions, there are some things we need to know before we can start adding materials to our scene.

The first is how to add a material. In previous versions of Blender, we could add a material using either the **Material** menu or the **Edit** menu. With Blender v2.50, we learned that this has been consolidated to one location—the **Material** menu. Remember, there are many parameters we can adjust to customize our materials, including:

- The material name and type
- Preview
- Diffuse and specular
- Shading
- Transparency and mirror
- Subsurface scattering

We learned how to add materials to our tricycle and how to customize them to better simulate how real materials look in the world around us. We made metal materials, plastic materials, and rubber materials that contained many realistic properties, resulting in a high quality render.

We also took a look at how Blender renders the 3D world around our object and how we can change those settings to create a more appealing background for our scene.

Summary

We've discussed a lot about materials in Blender and how to apply them to our scene. We've learned:

- About the various settings found with Blender's materials, including how to create, duplicate, and add special effects such as transparency and reflections to our materials
- How to customize them to be used in our scene
- How to change World settings to create a more interesting render

Congratulations! We've completed the first scenario—an outdoor-style lighting project! Let's review what we've learned over the course of this project and take a look at our next challenge—indoor lighting!

Indoor Lighting: Setting Up

Now that we're familiar with how to light a scene with the characteristics of outdoor lighting, it's time to take the next step and look at lighting interior spaces. Many of the techniques we used to light our last scene will transfer to this project quite nicely. However, there are some important differences that we're going to have to discuss that are unique to interior lighting. We're going to take a look at:

- Setting up our scene for use with a complex lighting system
- Implementing a more complex lighting system
- Setting up lights to reflect artificial lights in our scene, intuitively

Let's get started!

The first few steps

Before we begin, we need to know what our scene looks like. If you haven't already, go to the website (http://www.cgshark.com/lighting-and-rendering) and download the file interior.blend from the **Interior Lighting** download section. This is the file we will be using over the course of this project.

If you open it, it should look similar to the following image:

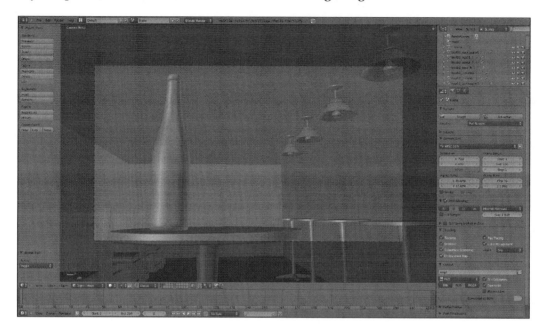

Diving in

Now that we have the right scene, let's get started. In the last project, the first step we learned was to evaluate our scene. In our case, we are really going to have to carefully consider how we're going to set up our lights. Let's take a moment and take a look at that now.

Enhancing our render using layers

With more complex scenes, Blender's layer system becomes an invaluable tool for lighting. Many times, we'll find that there are some objects that need unique lighting setups that aren't necessarily needed for the entire scene. To set up those unique "mini" light rigs, we need to link certain lights to specific layers, which we learned how to do in the last project. But we have a problem—right now, our scene is all on one layer. This means, we have to decide how we want to break up the objects in our scene so we can light them properly.

Let's take a quick look

Before we begin, we need to figure out what kind of mood we want to set. For this scene, we're going to want to focus on the wine bottle in the foreground, muting the background a bit using darker lighting and a slight change in focus. This will make the wine bottle the most prominent aspect of our scene.

Now, let's figure out where our light will primarily be coming from. We have two physical sets of light sources in our scene—the hanging lamps on the right and the embedded ceiling lamps on the left. We can use Spot lamps to simulate the hanging lamps on the right, and for the others, we can use Area lamps. Note that these Blender lamps aren't visible in the Blender file; in fact, they don't even exist yet. We are going to add them together later in the chapter.

Adding these lamps will light a good majority of our scene, but we still need to light the wine bottle in a way that makes it stand out from the rest of the scene. Because this is the focus of our scene, we're going to use a completely separate light to light it. In order for us to separate these light rigs properly, we're going to need to set up our scene in layers.

Organizing our layers

In the real world, objects we see are affected by all available sources of light. In computer graphics, though, we have complete control over how light affects our scene, and as a result, we have the artistic liberty to create effects with light that may not necessarily occur in a naturally-lit scenario for the sake of visual appeal. In Blender, we can separate our light sources using three-dimensional layers, which behave in the same way as layers in Adobe Photoshop or the GIMP. By default, Blender assigns every new object we create to the first layer, but we can move these objects around to fit the needs of our scene.

Deciding which layers to use solely depends on the preferences of the user and the needs of the scene. As long as the layers are used in a way that produces the desired result in the render, there is no "wrong" way to use them. Let's take a look at how we can use layers in our own scene!

We know we need to light our wine bottle separately. This means that we need to have, at the very least, the wine bottle and the table it's on, placed on a layer of their own. For logic's sake, we're going to leave these two on the first layer to start. Because the wine bottle is the focus of the scene, it makes sense to have it on the primary layer. Because we're not sure whether or not we're going to need to break up our scene further, let's place everything else in our scene on the layer directly below the first layer on the **Move to Layer** dialog box. That's probably confusing to take in all at once, so here's an image to help you.

To do this, follow these steps:

1. Select everything in our scene, except for the wine bottle and the table it's on.

 The easiest way to do this is to select everything in our scene, with the exception of the camera, and then deselect the wine bottle and table.

2. Press the *M-hotkey* to bring up the **Move to Layer** dialog box.
3. Select the layer button directly below the current layer (the first layer).

This moves everything selected to the designated layer.

Let's assume for a moment that we're going to use a 3-Point light rig to light our wine bottle similar to the light rig we used for the tricycle in our last project. This means that we're going to want our key light to light both the wine bottle and the table. We need this light to affect the table so we can render any shadows cast by the wine bottle.

The side light and rim light, on the other hand, only need to affect the wine bottle itself, not the table. This means we're going to have to move the table once more, this time to layer two. Following the same steps we used to move our objects the first time, select the table and move it to the second layer. The second layer is the layer button directly to the right of the first layer button.

Let's take a moment and quickly review what we've done. As of now, we should have:

- Moved everything in our scene, with the exception of the wine bottle, the table underneath the wine bottle, and the camera to the layer directly below the first layer button in the **Move to Layer** dialog box
- Moved the table once more from layer one to layer two

Turning theory into practice

We have a vision for our scene and we know how we're going to implement that vision. Now, all that's left to do is to do it. We're going to break this down into smaller steps—this lighting system is going to become fairly complicated fast, and the last thing we want is to get confused and all turned around. Let's break down the rest of the lighting section of this project into the following steps:

1. Set up the general rig. This includes lamps for the hanging light sources and the ceiling lights. We're not going to worry about light color at this point. With a light rig this complex, we're going to want to make sure first and foremost that the light intensity is balanced well before we start worrying about the details.
2. Set up the 3-Point rig for the wine bottle and table.
3. Set the lamp colors and set the ambient lighting settings, if applicable.
4. Tweak until satisfied.

Setting up the general rig

This step is by far the most straightforward step for this project. We are simply going to place lamps directly on top of the already existing three-dimensional models in our scene.

Adding Spot lamps

To start with, let's set up the lights for the hanging lights on the right side of our composition. We're simply going to create, position, and edit one light, then duplicate it to fit the rest of the lights.

1. Change into the Top view and make sure you're in wireframe mode by pressing the *Z-hotkey*.
2. Add a Spot lamp by selecting **Add | Lamp | Spot**.

3. Using the *G-hotkey*, position it so it's directly in the middle of the lampshade of the hanging light closest to the camera. Refer to the following image for help:

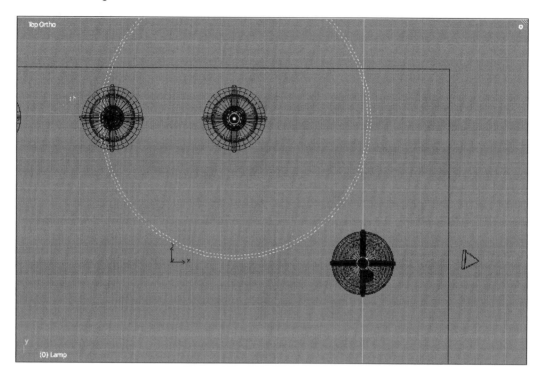

4. Change into either the front or right view and adjust the lamp so that it's positioned at the top of the shade, right below the support, as shown in the following screenshot:

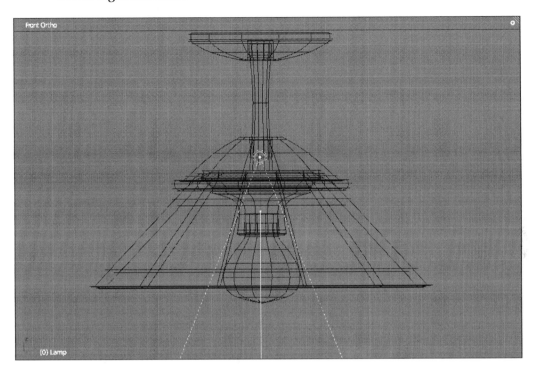

Before we continue, make sure that this lamp is on the same layer as the hanging lamps are. This would be the layer found directly below the first layer in the **Move to Layer** dialog box. If it's not already on the right layer, move it using the *M-hotkey*.

Now we need to adjust some lamp settings to better fit our light source. The first thing we need to change is the cone angle of our Spot lamp. Take a look at any real-life lamps that have shades similar to this one — the light follows the shape of the lampshade. This effect is most noticeable when a lamp is placed next to a flat surface, such as a wall.

To change this setting in Blender, make sure our lamp is selected and go to the
Light menu.

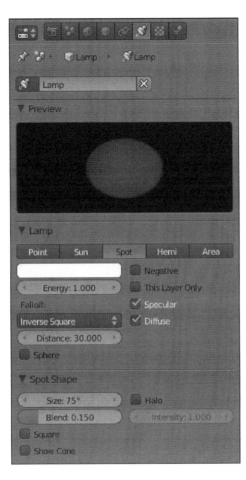

Under the **Spot Shape** settings, there's a parameter called **Size**. This controls the angle of the cone, which is set to 45 degrees, by default. Adjust this setting until the edges of the cone run parallel with the edges of the lampshade. It should look similar to the following image:

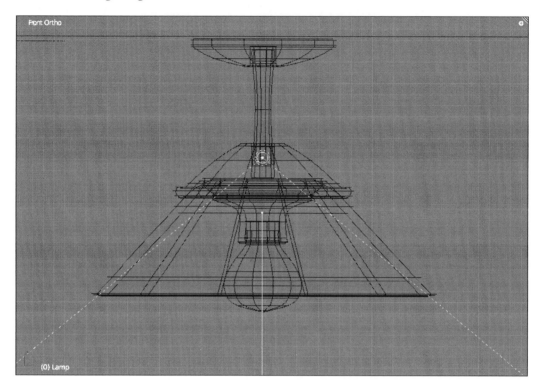

The angle of the cone in the image above is set to 102 degrees, but it may vary slightly, depending on where exactly the lamp is placed.

The next step is to change the **Blend** setting—this setting tells Blender how soft or hard to render the edges of the light on a surface. Our goal is to create a nice, soft edge. For now, set the value at 0.4. This should create a nice enough effect for what we're looking for. We also want to change the **Energy** setting to 0.7. Remember, earlier we decided to incorporate a darker background to make our wine bottle in the foreground pop forward.

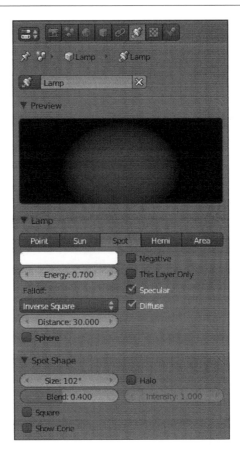

The final step is to adjust the **Shadow** settings. By default, Blender renders ray-traced shadows with Spot lamps, but we want to change this to buffer shadows. Because the area of our scene that will be lit by this lamp will be in the background, we don't have to worry about getting high-quality results, so we can get away with the buffer shadow algorithm. This will also cut down on our render time, because Blender won't have to make all of the mathematically meticulous calculations that come with the ray-tracing algorithm. Under the **Sample Buffers** setting, perform the following:

1. Set the number of sample buffers to 4.

2. Set the **Size** to 1024.

3. Set the **Samples** to 5.

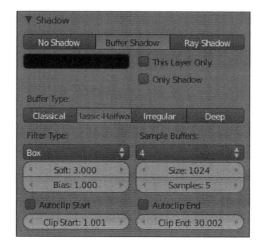

The last step is to select the **This Layer Only** option under the **Shadow** settings. This step is the key—if we don't choose this step, our lamp won't be linked to the layer. Although that isn't a huge problem right now, it will be if we don't set it up right with our 3-Point light rig, later in this chapter.

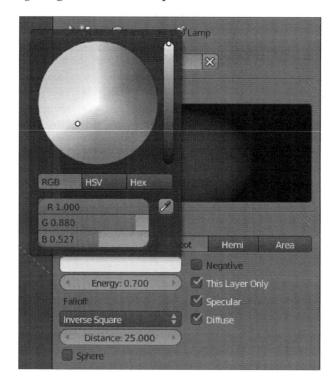

Now that we're finished customizing our first light, we can duplicate it to fit the remaining hanging light fixtures. To do so, follow these steps:

1. Select the Spot lamp.

2. Duplicate it by pressing the *Shift + D-hotkey* and transforming it along the x-axis until it lines up with the next lamp object. Your scene, from the front, should now look similar to the following screenshot:

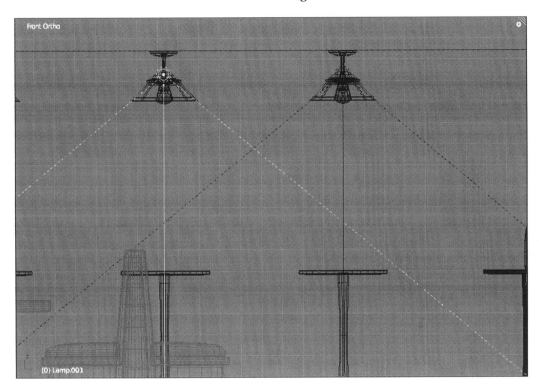

3. Repeat steps 1 and 2 until the entire row of hanging lamps is set up. Once that's done, we can move on to the other set of lights!

Let's take a look at how our scene looks so far. With only the Spot lamps lighting the scene, we get an effect similar to the following render:

Before we create our next lamp, we need to move the lampshades to another layer. With the lampshade selected (named `lamp_shade`), move it using the *M-hotkey* to the layer next to the layer it's currently on.

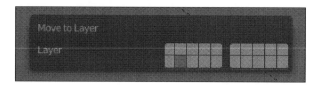

With the new layer selected, add a new Point lamp. This lamp will light the interior of our lampshade, giving it the impression that the light bulb is really affecting it. Move the new lamp using the *G-hotkey* so it's in the same place as our light bulb object. Also, change the color of this lamp to match the yellow hue Spot lamps we created earlier.

Before we render, we have to do three things. The first is link the lamp to the layer. To do this:

1. Without the lamp selected, select the **This Layer Only** option under the Lamp settings.

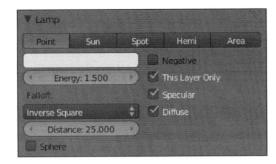

2. Next, turn on shadows by selecting **Ray Shadow** underneath the **Shadow** settings. The default values are fine.

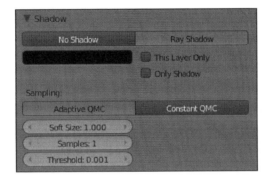

3. Like we did with the Spot lamp, duplicate our new lamp and move it so it fits under every hanging lamp.

Now let's render out our image!

It's a good start! Let's add some more lamps!

Setting up Area lamps

The second set of lights can be approached in the same way the first set was. The biggest difference between the two is the type of lamp used. Because the lights above the booths are held in rectangular casings, the best lamp we can use to simulate this is an Area lamp. This can be done by performing the following steps:

1. Change into the Top view.

2. Add an Area lamp by selecting **Add | Lamp | Area**.

3. Position it using the *G-hotkey* so it's placed directly above the booth farthest right. Also be sure to change into the Front or Right view to make sure the lamp is facing downward and positioned as close to the ceiling as possible. Refer to the following image for help:

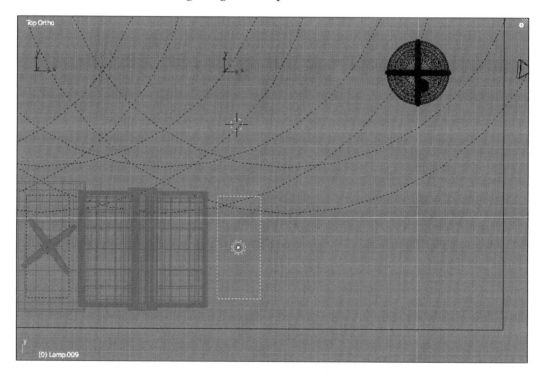

Although there isn't a table at the far right booth, the viewer assumes that our scene expands beyond the frame of our image. This means that we need to create the illusion that our scene continues beyond our render by adding this lamp.

As with our Spot lamp, we're going to duplicate our Area lamp so we can preserve our settings—this way, we don't need to repeatedly set the same settings. Before we do this, though, make sure it's on the same layer as our Spot lamps by selecting the lamp and moving it to the proper layer using the *M-hotkey*. Now to start, we need to change the shape of the lamp to better reflect the shape of the actual light model. With the Area lamp selected, go to the **Lights** menu and take a look at the **Area Shape** settings.

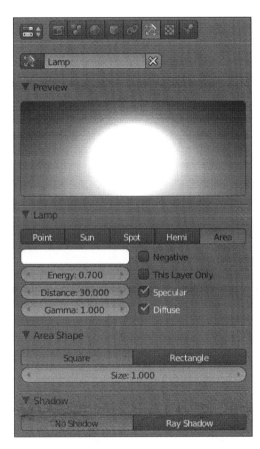

By default, Blender creates a square Area lamp, but we're going to want a rectangular one. To change this:

1. Click the **Rectangle** button.

Now, we have the **Size** controls for the size in the x-direction and the y-direction, not a single control for both.

2. Change the **Size X** parameter to 3 and the **Size Y** parameter to 7. These settings will suit our scene quite nicely.

The next thing to tackle is the light intensity. Area lamps are bright by default, but we want a somewhat dark background. This means we're going to have to change the **Distance** value of our lamp so that Blender renders it with the proper intensity. To do this, change the **Distance** value to 17.5 — this will change the **Distance** limit so that it reaches the floor. Also, set the Intensity value to 0.2.

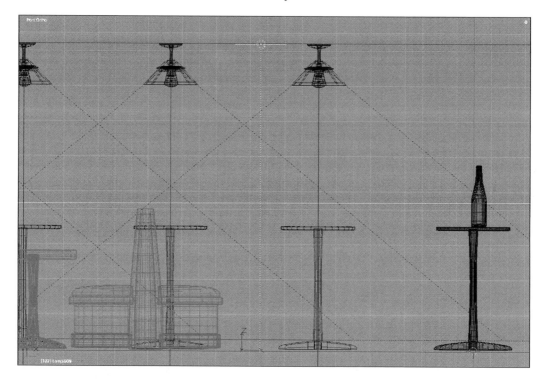

Area lamps don't support buffer shadows, so all we need to do is make sure **Ray Shadow** is selected under the **Shadow** settings. For our purposes, these defaults will be fine.

Just like we did with the Spot lamps, we need to make sure that the **This Layer Only** option is selected, so our lamps only light the objects on the same layer.

As with our other lamps, change the color to an orange hue. The values in the image below will work just fine.

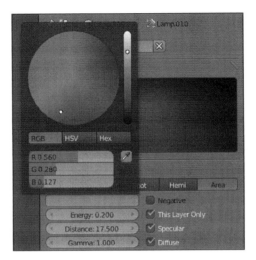

Now we can duplicate our Area lamp to finish up our general light rig! Using the *Shift-D-hotkey*, duplicate and position the new Area lamp so that it's aligned with the first table, as shown below:

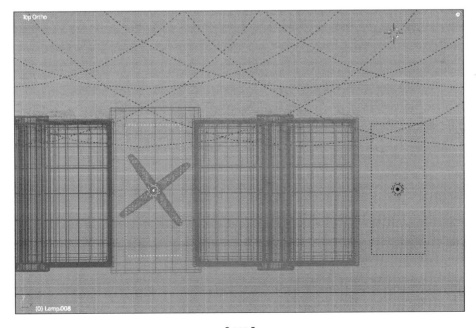

Continue duplicating the Area lamp until there's a lamp above each table in our scene. From the top view, our scene should now look something similar to the screenshot below:

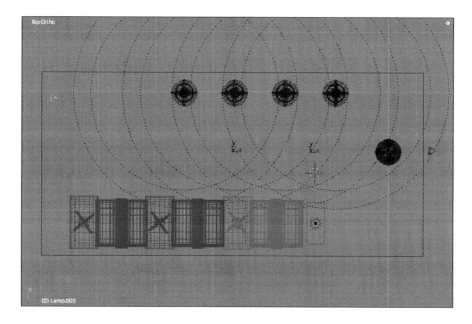

Render out the image as is—after large changes like this, it's always nice to check out the scene to make sure everything is working okay. Our scene should look similar to the following image, which is perfect for what we're going for

Adding ambient lighting

The next step is to add ambient lighting to our scene. We're going to use Blender's Environment Lighting feature to do this, and to set it up, we need to:

1. Activate **Environment Lighting** under the **World** menu by selecting the checkbox next to the setting.

2. Set the Energy value to 0.2. We don't want this too high, because this is an interior scene after all.

3. Activate Indirect Lighting as well (this will allow for some color bleeding and indirect illumination), and

4. Set the value to 0.4.

That's it! Easy enough, right? Let's see how it looks now! Note that because we have the ambient lighting algorithms running, this render may end up taking a while.

Lighting our wine bottle

Our background looks good, but we still need to light our wine bottle. Let's set up another light rig to do this. To start:

1. Add another Spot lamp.

2. Position it so it's to the left of our wine bottle in the image, just in front of it, and looking down on it at an extreme angle. Refer to the following screenshot:

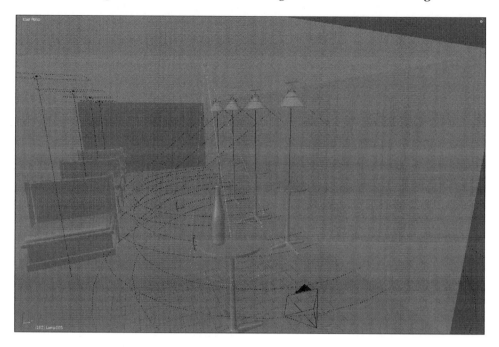

3. Change the color of our Spot lamp to another yellow hue, and
4. Change the Intensity to 4.0.

Let's check on our progress!

This setup looks pretty good. All we'll need to add now is a rim light to the bottle and we'll be set! To do so:

1. Add a sun lamp and make sure it's on the first layer with our wine bottle.

2. Position it so it's directly behind the bottle, facing toward the camera.

3. Move it to the first layer using the *M-hotkey*, so it's on the same layer as the bottle.

4. Select the **This Layer Only** option to link it to the first layer.

5. Render out the image, and we should have something similar to the following screenshot:

Summary

We've talked about a lot in this chapter. We've talked about:

*   Setting up a scene for use with a complex light rig by separating our scene into separate layers

*   Constructing a complex light rig

*   Linking lights to specific layers

*   Indirect lighting and how to integrate it with our scene

Next, we're going to talk about creating custom textures for our scene and how to bring them into Blender!

6
UV Mapping and Texturing

Many times, objects contain numerous attributes that define how they look, and they're not always perfectly uniform in relation to the object. For example, a used paint can would have paint dripping down the sides of the can—if we were creating this can in 3D, we'd have to tell Blender that there is a specific spot on our 3D mesh that contains different attributes than the rest of the mesh. This is where UV mapping comes in handy. UV coordinates are, in simple terms, a two-dimensional representation of the texture coordinates of a three-dimensional object. They allow us to tell Blender specific properties about specific areas of our objects in a scene.

Imagine a bearskin rug for a moment. In order to create that rug, someone had to take the skin and unfold it from its original place on the bear's body so that it fit nicely on a floor. This is essentially what we are doing when we create UV maps from our 3D objects. Using special tools in Blender, we can "unwrap" the UV coordinates so that they lay out flat on a two-dimensional plane, just like our bearskin rug.

To explore Blender's UV mapping tools, we're going to unwrap the wine bottle mesh. This is a perfect example for a few reasons. First, our wine bottle contains numerous material properties—not only will we need to create the overall glass material of the bottle, there's going to be a label running around the bottle as well. In order to position it correctly, we can use custom-made textures and map them to the wine bottle's UV set. Sounds confusing? It might, but let's open up our lit indoor scene and dive in. It'll make sense in no time!

Make sure you have your most recent copy of this scene open. If you want, visit http://www.cgshark.com/lighting-and-rendering and download the pre-built scene, complete with lights called indoor_lights.blend.

Changing our interface

Because of Blender's non-blocking interface, it's really easy to create custom interface layouts optimized for different aspects of production. Luckily for us, Blender's developers provide us with seven pre-made layouts optimized for the main aspects of film and game production:

- Animation
- Compositing
- Default
- Game logic
- Scripting
- UV Editing
- Video Editing

You probably didn't know Blender was capable of so much! As the Blender Foundation has proven with their open movie projects, Blender is fully capable of producing a game or animation without the help of other third-party programs (with the exception of an image manipulation program such as GIMP or Photoshop). To view these layout options, click the button to the left of the layout name at the top of the program window — refer to the image below for reference:

We are only concerned with the **Default** and **UV Editing** layouts right now. The **Default** layout is the layout we see when we open Blender for the first time — it's typically good for modeling and other basic tasks. Right now though, we're going to want to switch to the **UV Editing** layout, because this is a layout designed for UV mapping. To do so, we can do one of two things:

1. Using the layout menu, select the **UV Editing** layout option.

2. Use the *Ctrl+Right Arrow* shortcut. This loops through the available layout options. To find the **UV Editing** layout, continue to press *Ctrl+Right Arrow* until Blender's interface looks similar to the following image:

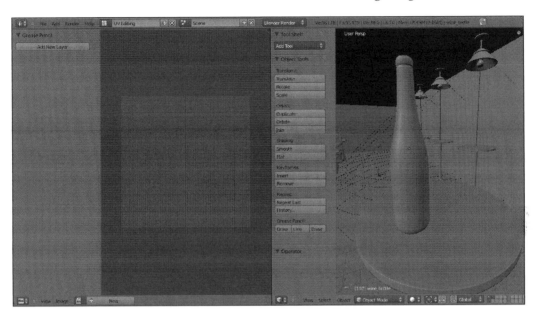

This is the default **UV Editing** layout. It contains the UV Image Editor on the left and the 3D view on the right. While editing our wine bottle's UV set, we will primarily be working on this layout to keep our interface neat and our minds at ease.

UV basics: marking a seam

Blender 2.5 supports numerous pre-defined projection algorithms that can be used to unwrap a 3D object, including:

- Cube projection
- Cylinder projection
- Sphere projection
- Project from view

Each of these projection algorithms are based on optimized settings that would be used to effectively unwrap objects such as cubes, cylinders, and spheres respectively. Imagine how we would peel the skin off of an orange—it may take multiple "cuts" to effectively peel the orange properly. Although these pre-defined project algorithms are nice, sometimes it's more useful to manually unwrap our objects. This is mostly used when working with organic models such as faces and other body parts, but it will work just as well for our wine bottle. Before we can unwrap our 3D mesh though, we need to create what's known as a **texture seam**. A texture seam acts in the same way the seam of a shirt does—it's the point on our mesh where the edges of our texture meet.

To create our seam, we need to first select the edges we want to use to define our seam with. With the wine bottle in Edit mode, select any vertical row of vertices like the image below—the easiest way to do this is to change into the Top view and select the vertices that way.

 We can also use the *Alt-Right-click* keyboard combination to select the column of vertices.

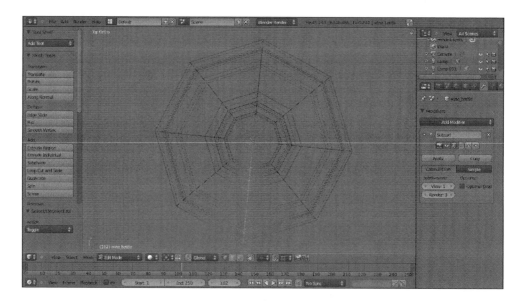

Now that we have our vertices selected, we need to tell Blender to turn them into a texture seam. With our vertices selected, hit the *Ctrl+E hotkey*—this brings up the **Edges** menu. Select the **Mark Seam** option, telling Blender to turn our vertices into a texture seam. If it was successful, our texture seam should be defined in the 3D view by a red border.

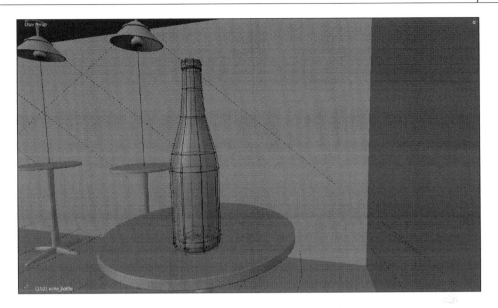

Unwrapping our mesh

After we have our texture seam, we can go ahead and tell Blender to *unwrap* our mesh. To do so:

1. Select all vertices.

2. Press the *U-hotkey* to bring up the **UV Unwrapping** menu.

3. Select **Unwrap**.

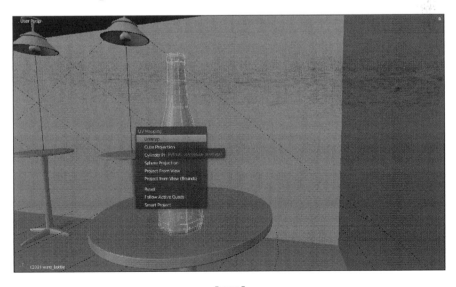

If we take a look at our UV Editing layout now, we will see that the Image Editor is showing our unwrapped UV set.

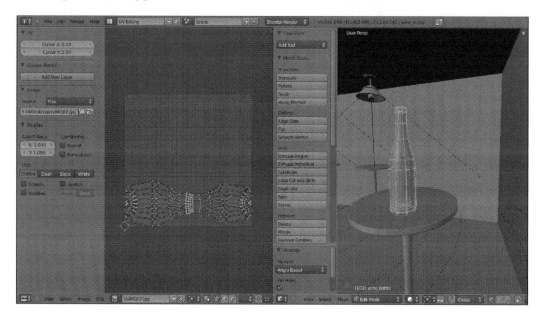

Cleaning up the UV map

Blender has already done a pretty good job at unwrapping our wine bottle, but we still need to work it so it has a more uniform shape. Blender provides a wonderful set of tools we can use to do this—in fact, Blender is well-known for its UV mapping capabilities.

To start, we need to rotate our UV map so it's facing upright. To do so, we can use the same hotkeys that we use in our 3D window. To rotate the UV map:

1. Select all of the UVs using the *A-hotkey*.

2. Press the *R-hotkey* and type -90 to rotate the UV coordinates 90 degrees counter-clockwise.

After rotating, our UV coordinates should be oriented similar to the following image:

Fine-tuning transformations

Sometimes it's necessary to tell Blender specifically how far you want to transform an object. To do this, we can select the transform we want to perform (move, rotate, or scale) by pressing their respective hotkeys—the *G-hotkey*, the *R-hotkey*, or the *S-hotkey*. Before finalizing the transformation with a mouse click, we can type the units we want to transform our object by.

For example, if we want to rotate our UV coordinates, we hit the *R-hotkey* and immediately after type -90. This tells Blender to rotate the UV map 90 degrees in the counter-clockwise direction.

To keep everything neat and clean, go ahead and move the UV map so it fits neatly inside the Image Editor. We need to do this because, in computer graphics, 3D programs map textures onto a mesh based on how the UVs are positioned within this UV space—Blender represents this space using the Image Editor. If any UVs are outside of the UV space, the program will not render our texture correctly. Depending on the program and the settings we have set, the image may show the texture repeating itself, or it may not show up at all. To avoid these issues, it's best to keep our UVs within this UV space.

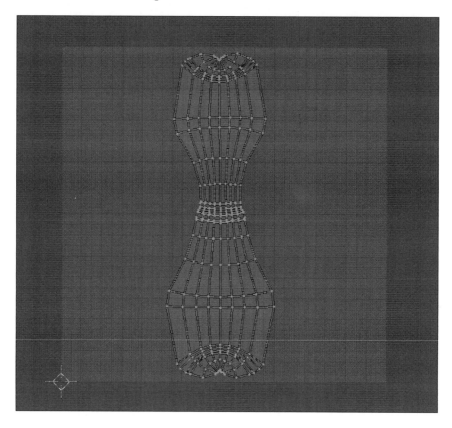

Blender's UV editing tools

Blender provides a bunch of tools we can use to work our UV map. The one we are going to utilize the most is called the **Align** tool. It takes all of the UV coordinates we have selected and aligns them along either the X or Y-axis.

Let's start by moving our UV map all the way over to the right of the Image Editor and select the column of UV coordinates.

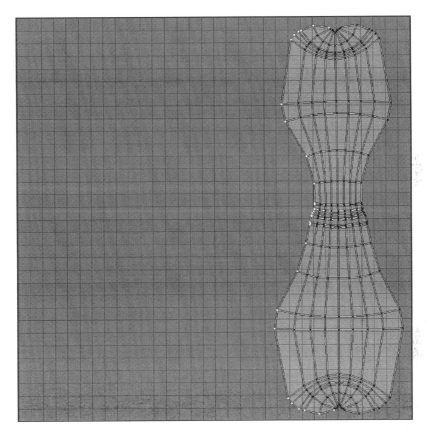

With the far left column of UV coordinates selected, make sure the mouse is in the Image Editor window and press the *Spacebar*. This brings up Image Editor's **Toolbox** menu. Go to **UVs | Weld/Align**. These are the align tools that we will be working with—more specifically, the **Align X** and **Align Y** tools.

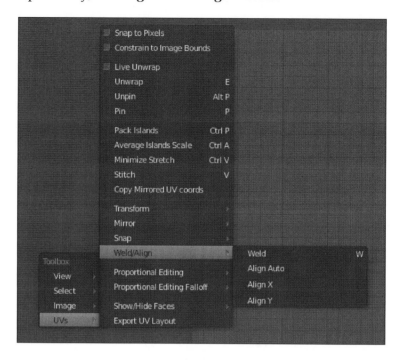

These tools take all selected UV coordinates and align them along either the X or Y-axis, depending on which option we choose. We can also access this menu directly by pressing the *W* key while our mouse is within the Image Editor.

Let's start by aligning each column in the X-direction. With the farthest left column of UV coordinates selected, move them along the X-axis to the opposite side of the Image Editor. To do this:

1. Press the *G-hotkey*, then immediately hit the *X* key to constrain movement to the X-axis.

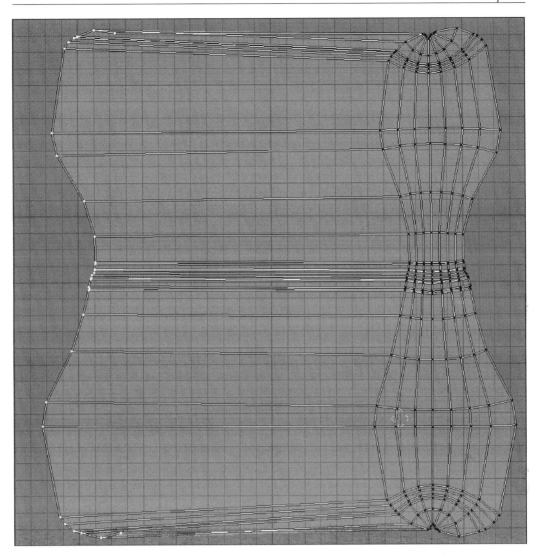

2. Use the **Align X** tool to align these UV coordinates along the X-axis.

3. Repeat Steps 1 and 2 until all columns of the UV map have been aligned along the X-axis. After we've finished, we should have something similar to the image below:

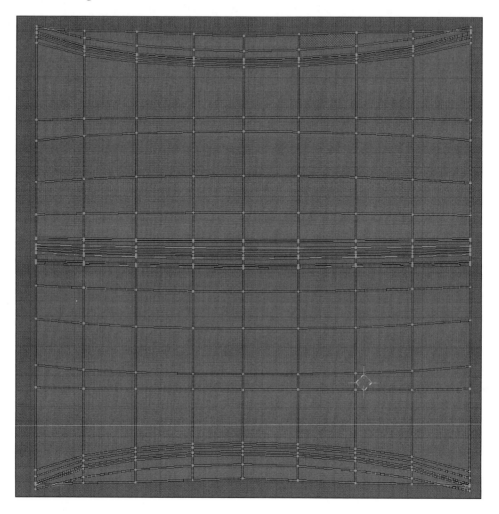

Now that the UV coordinates are aligned in the X-direction, we need to align them in the Y-direction. To do this:

1. Use the *G-hotkey* in conjunction with the *Y-key* to separate the top-most row of UV coordinates from the rest of the map. Move it up to the top of the Image Editor, away from the other coordinates.

2. Align the UV coordinates in the Y-direction by using the **Align Y** tool.

3.   Repeat Steps 1 and 2 until all columns are aligned.

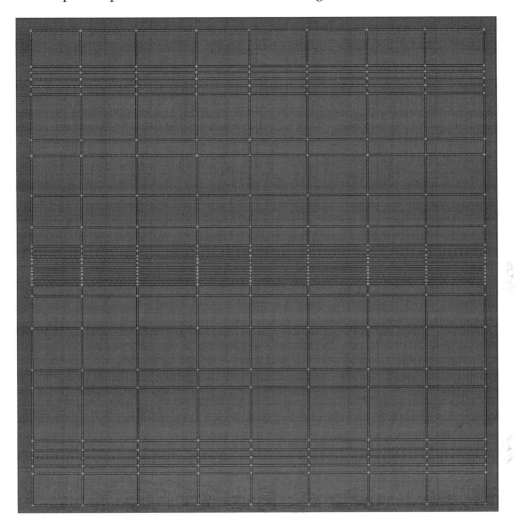

Using a reference image

Now that our UV map is, for the most part, uniform, we need to make sure that our UVs are proportional, so when we make our UV texture, it will render out correctly. The easiest way to do this is to use a material with a uniform pattern so we can identify any warping that shouldn't be there.

The most common kind of texture is a checkerboard, but we are going to use a more sophisticated version. Go to the website `http://www.cgshark.com/lighting-and-rendering` and download the texture named `uvhelp.jpg`. This texture not only has a checkerboard texture so we can look for warping, it also has numbers on it. Sometimes UV coordinates get flipped around, and the text allows us to see if our UV map is oriented in the right direction or not.

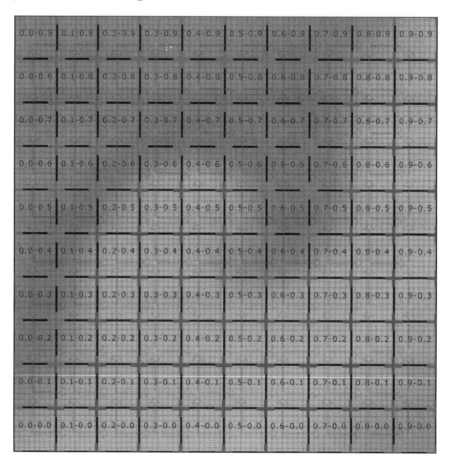

I'm going to let you in on a little secret—in order for us to view our wine bottle with this texture, we don't need to create a new material. In fact, we can do this directly in the Image Editor window. In the Image Editor, there's a string of menu options we can use—one of them controls the background image. To add a new image, go to **Image | Open**.

Navigate to the folder where you downloaded the reference image uvhelp.jpg. This will load the image into the Image Editor and effectively onto our mesh. But notice that although the image is visible in the Image Editor, it isn't visible on our mesh in the 3D view. This is because the 3D view is, by default, in a Shading view. We need to change the view to a Texture view by changing the Viewport Shading. Change the viewport from Shading to Texture and now we can see the checkerboard texture on our wine bottle.

Notice how some of the checkers are warped in the Y-direction. This means we have to move some of the rows along the Y-axis until the texture is no longer warped. Tweak the UV map for a while and see what happens. Once we fix the warping, our wine bottle should look something like the following image:

Creating a UV texture

Now that we have our UV map all set up, we can create a custom UV texture! But, before we can even do that, we need to export our current UV map from Blender to a file that an image manipulation program, such as GIMP or Photoshop, can read.

Exporting our UV map

Now that we have GIMP downloaded, we can export our UV map from Blender to a format that GIMP can read. To do this, make sure we can view our UV map in the Image Editor. Then, go to **UVs | Export UV Layout**.

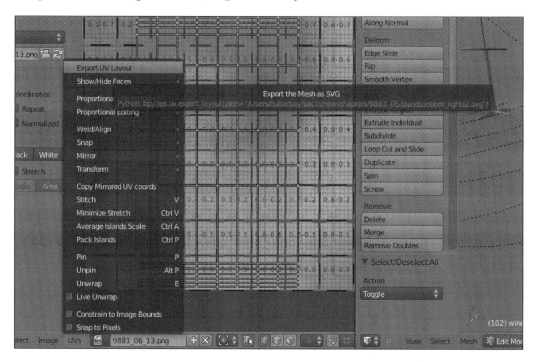

Then save the file in a folder you can easily get to, naming it UV_layout or whatever you like.

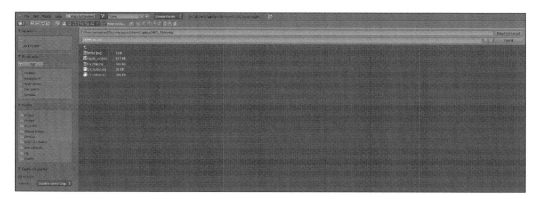

Now it's time to open GIMP!

Downloading GIMP

Before we begin, we need to first get an image manipulation program. If you don't have one of the high-end programs, such as Photoshop, there still is hope. There's a wonderful free (and open source) program called GIMP, which parallels Photoshop in functionality. For the sake of creating our textures, we will be using GIMP, but feel free to use whatever you are personally most comfortable with.

To download GIMP, visit the program's website at `http://www.gimp.org` and download the right version for your operating system.

Mac Users will need to install X11 so GIMP will run. Consult your Mac OS installation guide for instructions on how to install.

Windows users, you will need to install the GTK+ Runtime Environment to run GIMP—the download installer should warn you about this during installation. To install GTK+, visit `http://www.gtk.org`.

Hello GIMP!

When we open GIMP for the first time, we should have a 3-window layout, similar to the following screen:

Create a new document by selecting **File | New**. You can also use the *Ctrl+N* keyboard shortcut. This should bring up a dialog box with a list of settings we can use to customize our new document.

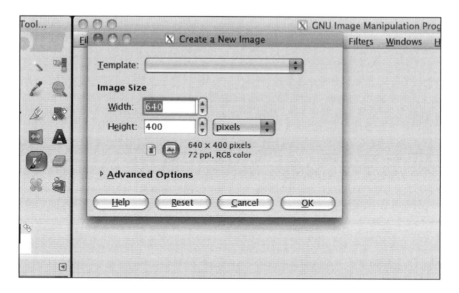

Because Blender exported our UV map as an SVG file, we can choose any size image we want, because we can scale the image to fit our document.

 SVG stands for **Scalable Vector Graphic**. Vector graphics are images defined by mathematically calculated paths, allowing them to be scaled infinitely without the pixilation caused when raster images are enlarged beyond a certain point.

Change the **Width** and **Height** attributes to 2000 each. This will create a texture image 2000 pixels wide by 2000 pixels high. Click on **OK** to create our new document.

Getting reference images

Before we can create a UV texture for our wine bottle, which will primarily define the bottle's label, we need to know what is typically on a wine bottle's label. If you search the web for any wine bottle, you'll get a pretty good idea of what a wine bottle label looks like. However, for our purposes, we're going to use the following image:

Matthew http://www.flickr.com/photos/falcon1961/3409770684/

Notice how there's typically the name of the wine company, the type of wine, and the year it was made. We're going to use all of these in our own wine bottle label.

Importing our UV map

A nice thing about GIMP is that we can import images as layers into our current file. We're going to do just this with our UV map. Go to **File** | **Open as Layers...** to bring up the file selection dialog box.

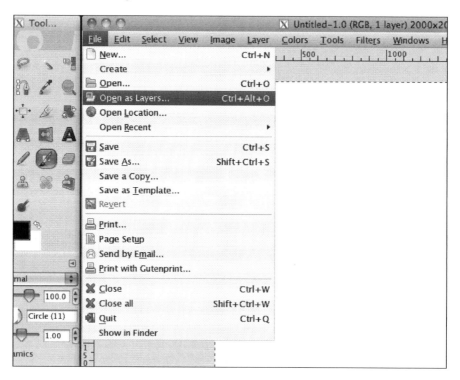

Navigate to the UV map we saved earlier and open it. Another dialog box will pop up—we can use this to tell GIMP how we want our SVG to appear in our document.

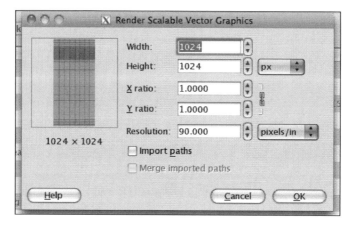

Change the **Width** and **Height** attributes to match our working document—2000px by 2000px. Click on **OK** to confirm.

 Not every file type will bring up this dialog box—it's specific to SVG files only.

We should now see our UV map in the document as a new layer.

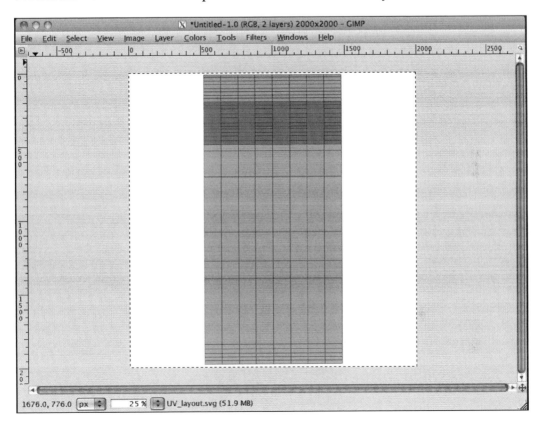

Before we continue, we should change the background color of our texture. Our label is going to be white, so we are going to need to distinguish our label from the rest of the wine bottle's material. With our background layer selected, fill the layer with a black color using the **Fill** tool.

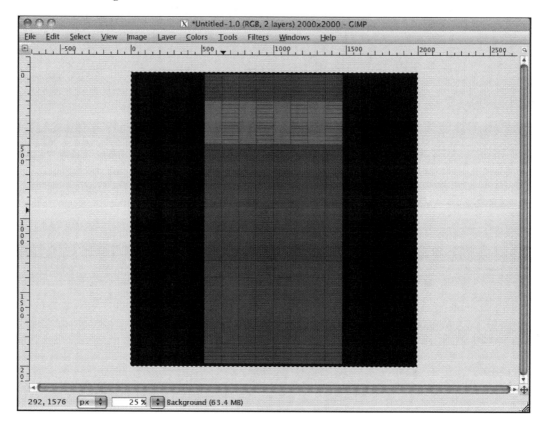

Next, we can create the background color of the label. Create a new layer by clicking on the **New Layer** button. Name it `label_background`.

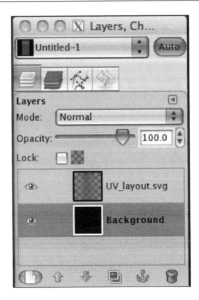

Using the **Marquee Selection** tool, make a selection similar to the following image:

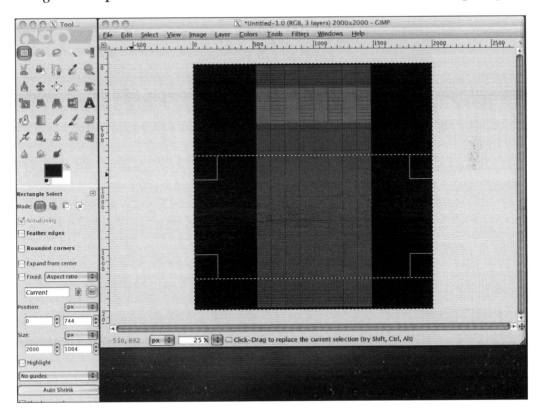

Fill it, using the **Fill** tool, with white. This will be the background for our label—everything else we add with be made in relation to this layer.

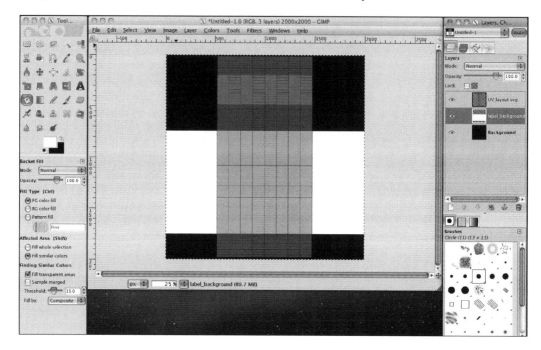

 Keep the UV map layer on top as often as possible. This will help us keep a clear view of where our graphics are in relation to our UV map at all times.

Adding text

We're almost there! All we need to do is add some text. Before we do that, though, we want to make sure that our text is centered with our image. To do that, we need to add Guides in GIMP. To create a Guide, simply click on one of the rulers to the side of our image and drag.

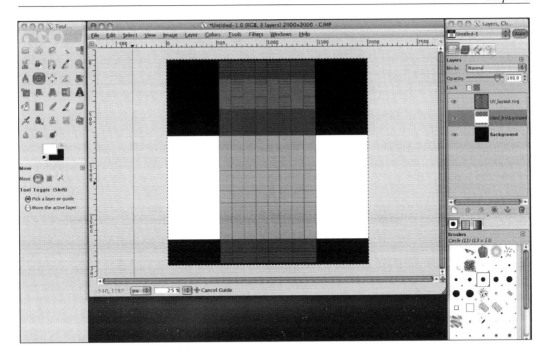

Move the Guide until it's positioned 1000 pixels from both sides. We will use this to align our text.

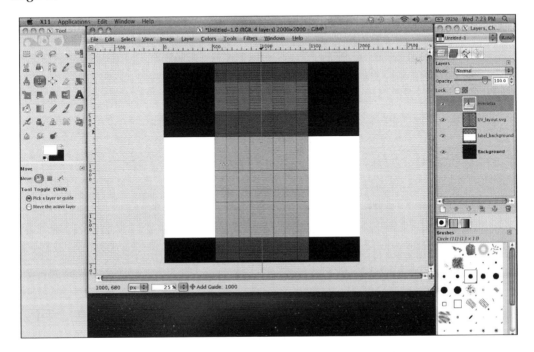

To start, we need to create some title text for our wine bottle. For this tutorial, we are going to use the name Henrietta Blue. We want to create a feeling of elegance, so let's look for a font with curves and serifs. We're also going to want to use a different color for the word Blue to emphasize it, so we're going to have to use two separate text layers for the title—unlike Photoshop, GIMP doesn't support using multiple colors on one text layer.

Using the **Text** tool:

1. Click within our image to add a new text layer.
2. Type the word Henrietta.
3. Change the font size to 68.
4. Change the font color to black.

   Now we need to change the font to one that suits our needs. Change the font to the one you choose earlier—in our case, I'm going to use Didot Italic.

5. Change the font to Didot Italic (or the font of your choosing).
6. Move the font so it matches the position in the image below:

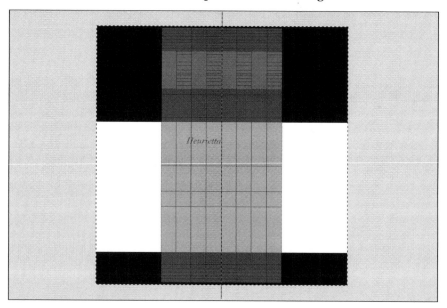

Save often!

Before we continue, we should save. Make frequent saves to avoid losing work. In GIMP, go to **File | Save As** and save the image as UV_texture.xcf. XCF is GIMP's extension for files, comparable to Photoshop's PSD file type.

Now let's continue...

Now that we're sure our file is safe, let's continue. Duplicate the `Henrietta` text layer and move it over so it's on the opposite side of the Guide. Our image should now look like the following image:

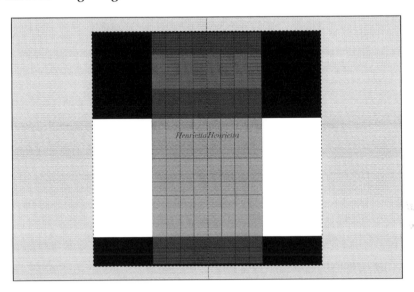

But, remember our wine is called "Henrietta Blue", not "Henrietta Henrietta". Using the Text tool again, edit the text of our new text layer so it reads `Blue`. Then, change the color of the text to a blue hue—we can use the hex value `#49a4e3`.

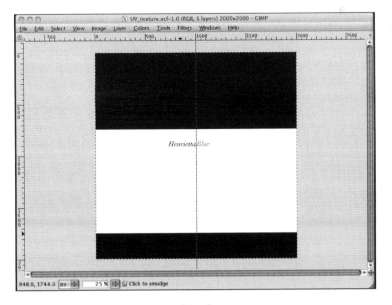

Next, we need to create a logo for our wine brand. For this logo, we're going to use the design found on the flag of the Republic of Kosovo—make sure it's downloaded from the website at `http://www.cgshark.com/lighting-and-rendering`.

Now that we have our "logo", we need to import it as a new layer into GIMP. To do this:

1. Press **File | Open As Layers**.

2. Navigate to the folder where we downloaded the "logo" image.

3. Press **Open**.

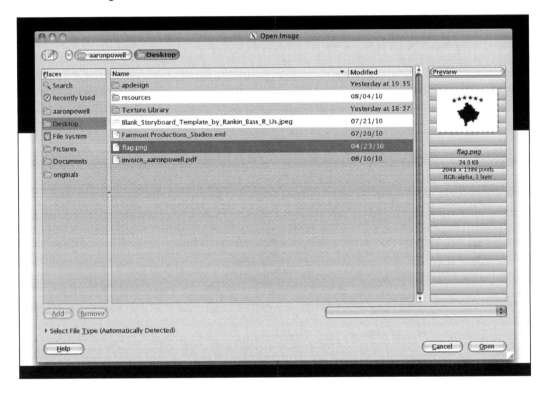

Now we can see that our "logo" has been brought into GIMP as its own layer! Let's position it so it's directly below our Henrietta Blue text. To do this:

1. Make sure GIMP's **Move** tool is selected and click and drag our "logo" until it is positioned underneath our Henrietta Blue text, centered with the image.

2. If needed, use the **Scale** tool to make the logo smaller, so that it fits within our whitespace.

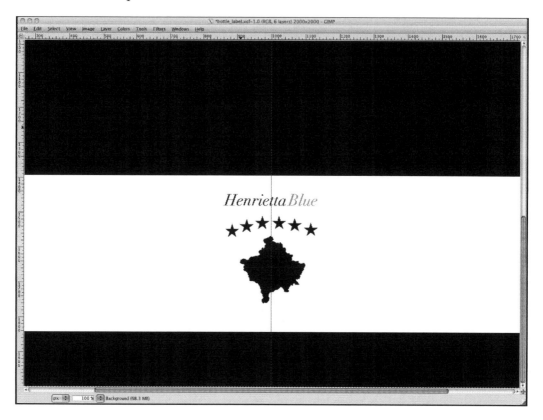

Our last step is to add what kind of wine our bottle contains. This can be whatever you choose—for the sake of this lesson, we're going to make it champagne. Using the text tool, create a new text layer with the word "champagne", written in all-caps. Adjust the font so it's a nice serif font, like the one below:

Now all we have to do is position it properly and we're done! Using the **Move** tool, position the word champagne so it's centered underneath our logo.

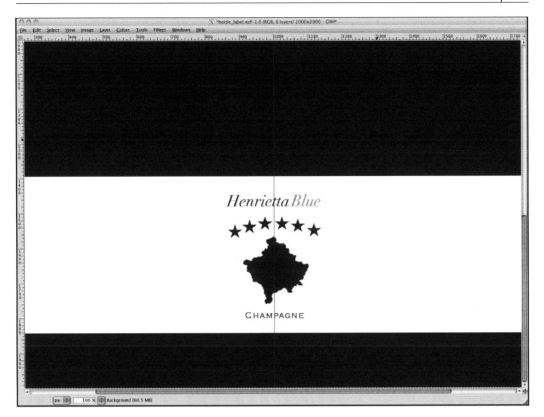

Summary

We've learned a lot about Blender's UV capabilities and how we can use them to create custom UV textures for our scenes. We have taken a look at:

- Marking a texture seam
- Unwrapping a mesh
- Cleaning up UV meshes
- Exporting UV meshes for use in image manipulation software
- How to use a program like GIMP to create a custom texture for our 3D scene

Next, we're going to look at how we can pull our new custom texture back into Blender, so we can use it in our 3D render!

7

Indoor Lighting: Finishing Materials

Now that we've created a custom UV map for our wine bottle, we can finish texturing our scene. Because our wine bottle is made up of numerous materials with different qualitites, it's important to know how we can set up our material so Blender will render it properly. We're also going to take a look at:

- Exporting our UV map as a file type which Blender can read
- Adding our UV map to the wine bottle mesh
- Adding materials for the rest of the objects in our scene
- Tweaking the final render

Setting up project folders

One thing we haven't talked about yet is the concept of project folders. As we start dealing with more and more complicated scenes, it will be essential to create a project folder to organize all of our project assets. These include, but certainly aren't limited to:

- Blend files
- Reference images
- Textures
- Scripts (if applicable)
- Renders

An easy way to organize these files is by their file type. For example, we can set up a project folder for our current scene.

1. Create a new folder and name it `indoor_lighting`.

2. Open our newly created folder and create four new folders again, naming them `images`, `references`, `scenes`, and `renders`. We will use these folders to organize our project assets.

3. Move our `working.blend` file into the scenes folder—this folder will contain all Blender files we make over the course of this project.

Now that we have a project folder set up, we can go ahead and start to work more on our materials and textures!

Exporting our UV map

Before we can bring our UV map into Blender, we need to save it as a file Blender can read. Blender supports all major file types, so we're going to play it safe and use the `.png` file type. Let's open up our UV map again in GIMP.

To save our texture as a `.png`:

1. Go to **File | Save As**.

2. Find the `images` folder we created earlier, inside our project folder.

3. Save the file as `bottle_label.png`.

Make sure you type `.png` at the end—one of the nice things about GIMP is that you can dictate the file type simply by typing it into the filename.

Creating materials using Blender's Compositor

Blender's Node Compositor is extremely useful for adding additional layers of dimension and effects to both our scene as well as our materials. We're going to take a look at how to use the Compositor to create the material for our wine bottle.

Creating a glass material

Open up our scene in Blender and select the wine bottle. We're first going to add our UV texture and then deal with other aspect of the material later such as the glass material of the bottle.

1. Under the **Material** menu, create a new material.

2. Name it `wine_bottle`.

We're going to use Blender's Node Compositor to combine the different materials found on our wine bottle. Remember when we changed our window layout to edit our wine bottle's UV coordinates? We're going to do the same thing here, but will choose the **Compositing** layout instead. Go ahead and change the layout now that our wine bottle has the material applied to it.

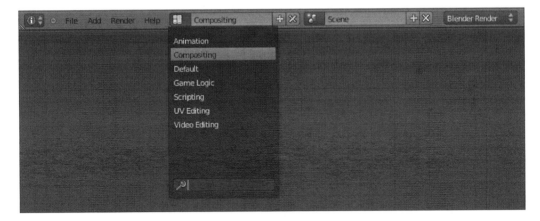

By default, Blender doesn't enable materials to be controlled by the Compositor—we'll have to do that manually. To use Blender's Node Compositor to manage our mesh, click the node toggle button found between the material name and the list that dictates how the material is linked to our object (by default, Blender sets this to **Data**).

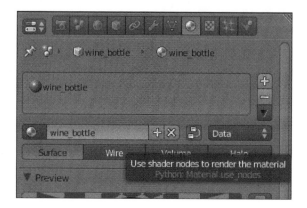

We'll notice that when we press this button, Blender automatically adds some nodes to the Compositor window—these will serve as a starting point for our **node network** or the network of linked nodes that define our material.

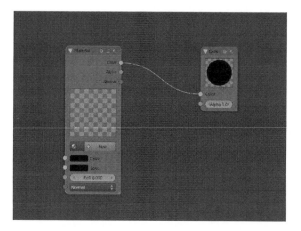

We're going to need to create two separate materials to use for our wine bottle material—one is a glass material, and the other is the label material. Let's start with the glass material. We already have a **Material** node in our node network, which we will use to create our glass material. Under the **Material** node, press the **New** button to create another material.

Rename this material `glass`. When a **Material** node is selected, we can adjust the settings under the **Material** menu to the right to edit that particular material's properties.

 Despite the **Material** node we have selected, the **Material** menu will always show the name of the material applied to our object—in our case, the `wine_bottle` material. Be sure you have the desired **Material** node selected when you start editing these values.

With our `glass` **Material** node selected:

1. Activate the **Transparency** values.
2. Change the algorithm from **Z Transparency** to **Raytrace**.

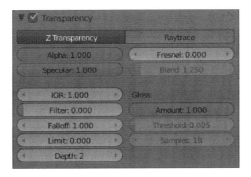

Most commercial-grade glass has an index of refraction, or **IOR**, of `1.55`. Because we want a `realistic` result, we can go ahead and use that value in Blender's **IOR** parameter.

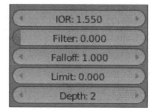

Realistic, though, is a relative term. Blender can't render raytraced transparency in the Compositor in the same way it does in a normal render, and as a result, it has to be faked. Although the result won't look bad, we can apply some tricks to hide those shortcomings later on.

We also need to edit the **Fresnel** value to set the proper transparency—for now, set it at a value of `3.0`.

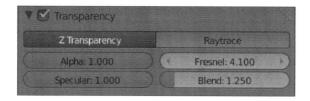

There's a problem, though. If we render out our image now, it's not exactly transparent. This is because although the material has transparency enabled, the alpha channel isn't linked to the materials output in the Compositor.

To do this, click on the small gray circle next to **Alpha** output on the glass **Material** node and drag over to the gray circle next to the **Alpha** input on the **Output** node. This will link the transparency values to the composited material.

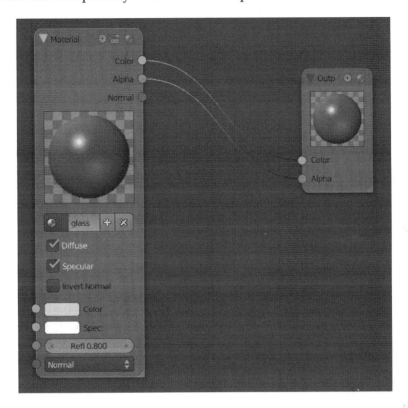

Now, if we render out our image, we will get a better transparency result. It's better, but not perfect yet.

Notice how the glass appears to be black—this is because the **Depth** parameter is not high enough. To improve the transparency quality, change this value to 6.

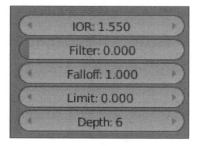

There's a noticeable difference between our renders now. With the **Depth** value at 6, we can actually see what appears to be a transparent glass bottle! Remember, though, it's not a "true" transparency, and as a result, it doesn't look entirely believable. We're about to take care of that, masking Blender's shortcoming with the **Gloss** parameter.

We're going to use the Gloss parameter to "blur" the fact that this transparency isn't entirely believable. To do this, set the **Gloss** value to 0.9.

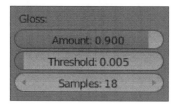

This effectively masks our transparency enough so that we can tell it's a transparent bottle, but we can't see that Blender faked the transparency.

The next step is to add some reflections. What is glass without reflections, anyway? To do this:

1. Activate the **Mirror** settings.
2. Set the **Reflectivity** value to 0.04.
3. Set the **Depth** value to 6.
4. Set the **Gloss** to 0.9.

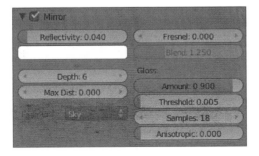

Although the effect of the reflection is minute, it's an effect that really adds to the believability of our glass material. With reflections added, our image should look similar to the following render:

We're making great progress! The last step for the glass material is to adjust some of the **Diffuse** and **Specular** settings. To start:

1. Adjust the **Diffuse** color to a gray-blue hue. Refer to the image below for specific RGB values:

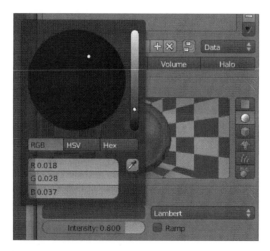

2. Adjust the **Specular** color so that it's an off-white color. Again, refer to the image below:

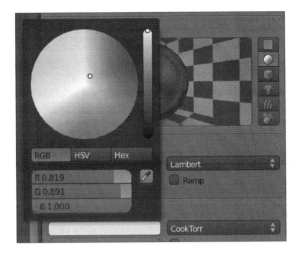

3. Set the **Specular Intensity** to 1.0.
4. Set the **Hardness** to 200.

Let's render out our image to check on our progress!

It doesn't look like much has changed. This is because our **Fresnel** parameter is set so high that it's letting more transparency than color through in our material. Lower this value to 2.15 and render the image again—we should get a much better result this time.

Creating a label material

To add our label, we're going to need to create another material that we can place on top of the glass material we just made. To do this, we need to create a new **Material** node. Create a new **Material** node by:

1. Selecting **Add | Input | Material** in the Compositor window.

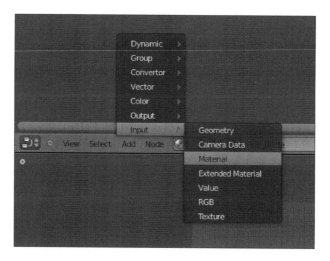

If there are any connections automatically assigned to our new **Material** node, drag the connection away from the node to disconnect it.

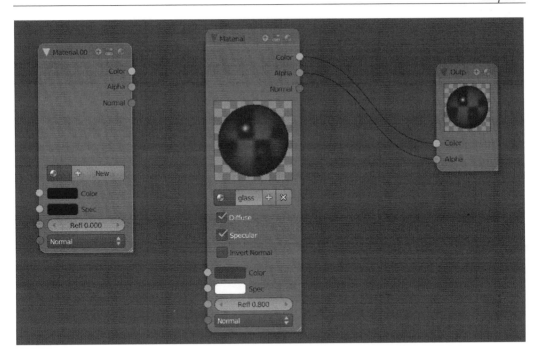

2.   As we did before, click the **New** button to create a new material.

3.   Rename it `label`.

     Because we want to use our UV map to define the color of our label, we need to create a **Texture** node to attach to the label **Material** node. Before we do this, though, we need to create the texture. Let's take a second and switch back into the **Default** screen layout.

     Navigate to the **Texture** menu.

4.   Create a new texture, naming it `label_image`.

5.   Change the texture type to **Image or Movie**.

6.   Load the UV map we created earlier, `bottle_label.png`, into the texture.

Now that our texture is created, we need to remove it from the current material so there aren't any conflicts with our node network later on. To do this, click the **X** button to the right of the texture name at the top of the menu.

That's it! Now we can change our screen layout back to Compositing to continue working with our node network. Now we can create a **Texture** node to use in our network. To do this:

1. Select **Add | Input | Texture** from the Compositor's menu.

2. Add our texture to the node by clicking on the blank box and selecting the texture `label_image` from the drop-down list.

Now we need to tell our texture to dictate the color of our `label` material. To do this, click and drag from the **Color** output on the **Texture** node to the **Color** input node on the **label Material** node.

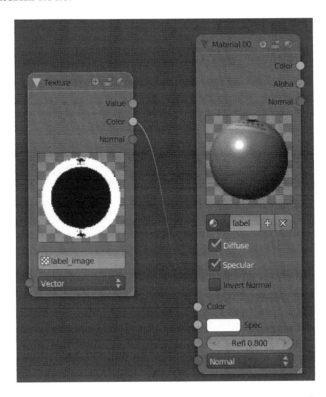

Now we can see that our texture has been applied to the material in the Preview box. The next step is to add the label to our glass material using a **Mix** node. To do this, select **Add | Color | Mix** in the Compositor window.

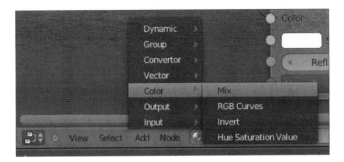

Click and drag the **Color** output channels from the **glass** material node and the **label** material node and attach them to the **Color1** and **Color2** input channels respectively. Blender layers nodes attached to **Color2** on top of nodes connected to **Color1**, which means our label will appear on top of the glass. Our network should now look something similar to the following screenshot:

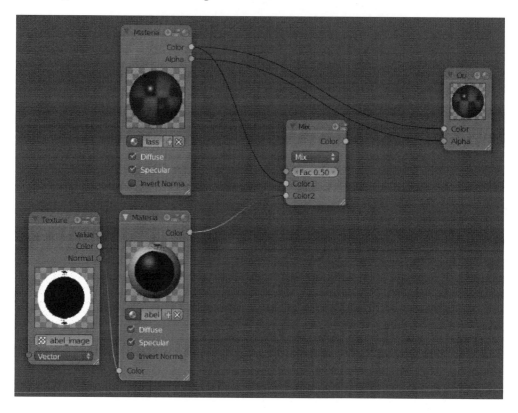

We now need to attach the **Mix** node to the Output node—otherwise Blender won't know to mix the two materials. Because the node channels can only accept one input connection at a time, Blender automatically disconnects the link between the glass material node's **Color** channel and the **Output** node's **Color** channel when we attached the **Color** channel from the **Mix** node.

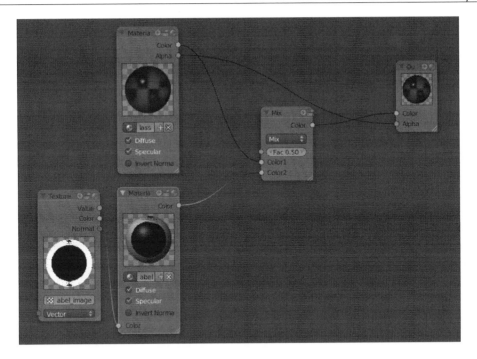

Now let's render our image out and see our result!

It looks okay, but there are still some minor details we have to tackle. The first is the label — there's still a reflection on the label part of the bottle from the glass material, even though there are no reflective properties of the label material itself. It's also improperly mapped, which we will deal with in a moment. We also can't see the blue color anymore, because Blender mapped the black color from the label texture on top of the glass material. We can use another texture to separate these materials so Blender renders them properly.

We're going to use the following image to separate, or mask, our materials. It's an edited version of the label image, just without the details of the label itself. You can create this image yourself, or you can download a copy from `http://www.cgshark.com/lighting-and-rendering/`. Select the `label_mask.png` image from the Interior Lighting project list.

Just like we did before, we need to create a new texture for this image. Switch to the **Default** screen layout and navigate to the **Texture** menu.

1. Create a new texture.
2. Rename it `label_mask`.
3. Change the Type to **Image or Movie**.
4. Load our newly downloaded image, `label_mask.png`.

Go ahead and remove the texture from the current material by clicking the **X** next to the name, and we can change back to the Compositing screen layout.

1. Add a new **Texture** node.
2. Click the blank box and select the texture `label_mask` from the drop-down list.
3. Click and drag to connect the Texture node's Color output to the Fac input on the **Mix** node.

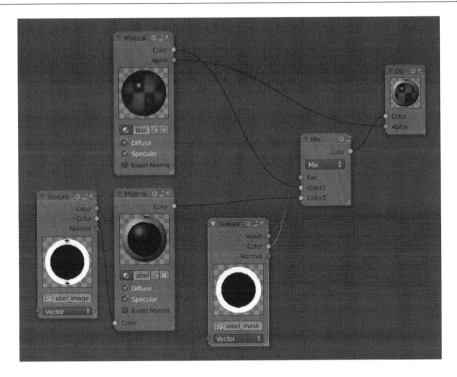

We can now use the node compositor to tell Blender to use the wine bottle's UV-coordinates to map our `label_image` and `label_mask` textures to our wine bottle so that they appear correctly in our render. We can use a Geometry node to do this—the Geometry node contains information about the object the material is connected to, including things like texture coordinates and other settings. To create a Geometry node:

1. Select **Add | Input | Geometry** in the Compositor window.

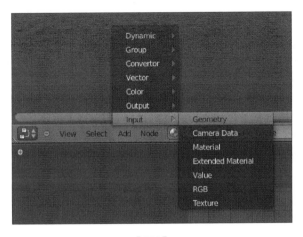

2. Connect the UV output of the Geometry node to the Vector inputs on both the `label_image` Texture node and the `label_mask` Texture node.

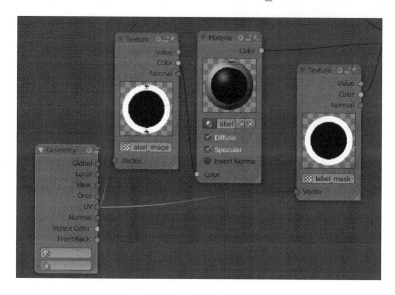

Now if we render our image out, the label should look a lot better.

The last thing we're going to do is soften the specular highlight on our label to make it more distinguishable from the glass material. To do this:

1. Select the `label` material node.

2. Set the **Hardness** value to 20.

3. Set the **Specular Intensity** value to 0.2.

Here's our final material node network.

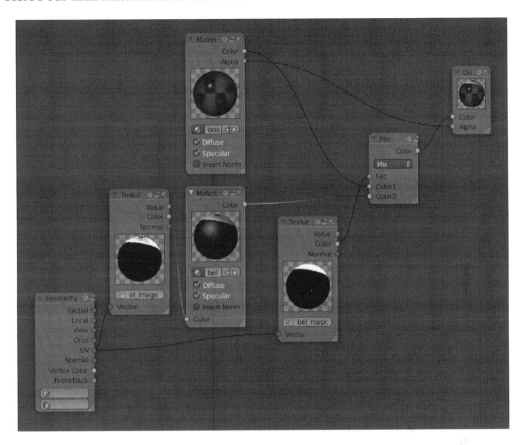

That's it! Our wine bottle is finally done! Now let's move on to the rest of the scene and finish adding materials.

Finishing up materials

Congrats! We've successfully completed our first UV-powered material! Now we're going to take a step back and finish up the rest of the scene. From here on, any images or UV maps we're going to use have been provided for us, so we don't have to worry about making them again.

Downloading images

Before we continue, let's make sure that we have all of the files we need for the rest of this scene. Go to the website (`http://www.cgshark.com/lighting-and-rendering`) and download the following images:

- `booth_color.png`
- `wallpaper_color.png`
- `table_color.png`
- `metal_bump.png`

Once we've downloaded them, we need to place them in the `images` folder we created earlier. If we do this now, we won't have to worry about losing the files when we actually need to use them.

Creating a wood material

Let's start by adding a wood material to the booths. Select the sideboard of the original booth mesh.

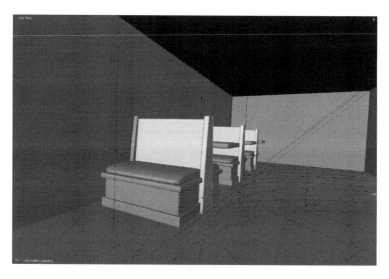

To add the wood material:

1. Under the **Material** menu, add a new material.

2. Name it `booth_wood`.

3. Leaving the material settings at their defaults and go to the **Textures** menu.

4. Add a new texture and name it `booth_color`.

This texture is going to dictate the color of our wood material. Change the **Type** to **Image or Movie** and load the `booth_color.png` image we downloaded earlier.

 Notice that the image name and the texture name match—this is a good habit to get into, especially when dealing with bigger projects.

The more organized our scene and scene assets are, the more it will make sense if we ever return to the scene later to work on it again. Change the name of the texture to `booth_color_file`.

By default, the **Preview** displays our texture on a sphere. Because our texture will be on meshes that have rectangular shapes, it makes more sense to preview it on a rectangular mesh as well. Change the **Preview** mesh to a cube.

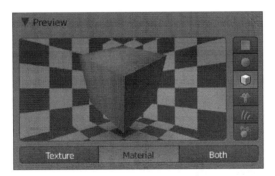

The next step is to change the mapping projection type. Under the **Mapping** settings, change **Projection** to **Cube**. This will map our image properly onto our rectangular-shaped object—using the default "Flat" projection would cause some distortion in our render.

Before we test our render, we're going to want to apply the material to the rest of the booth as well. To do this, select the remaining parts of the booth and add the material by clicking the icon to the left of the **New** button. Select `booth_wood`.

Let's test our render!

That's looking pretty good! Let's take a look at the wallpaper next.

Adding a wallpaper

Select the cube surrounding our scene to start—these are the walls of our render.

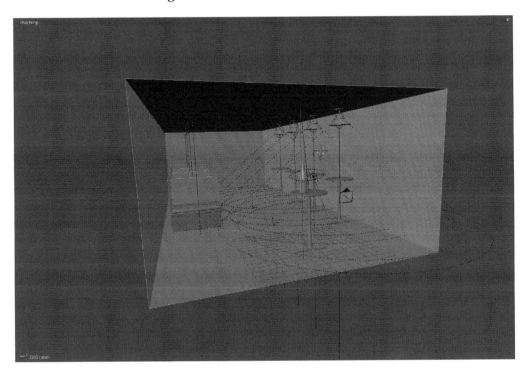

1. Under the **Material** menu, create another material, naming it `wallpaper`.

2. Go to the **Texture** menu and create a new texture.

3. Name the texture `wallpaper_color`.

4. Change the **Type** to **Image or Movie**.

5. Load the `wallpaper_color.png` image we downloaded earlier.

   Now that our image texture is loaded into Blender, we're going to have to change the **Mapping** settings. Because this is a UV-texture, we're going to have to tell Blender to use the mesh's UV map.

6. Under the **Mapping** settings, change the **Coordinates** to **UV**.

7. Select the layer named **UVTex**.

   Now our UV-texture is all set to go—there's just a couple more settings we have to change in the **Material** menu. By default, Blender renders materials with a moderate specular value. The walls of our room, though, don't have a very high specular value, so we're going to have to change those settings to match our room better.

8.   Under the **Material** menu, change the **Specular Intensity** to .05

9.   Change the **Hardness** to 10.

We also know enough about color theory to know that a material with a red diffuse color shouldn't have a pure white specular—not a material with such a low specular value at least. More likely than not, our walls will have a specular color value that's a slightly brighter red than the diffuse color of the wall itself. Using the color picker, change the specular color to a pinkish-red—refer to the image below for guidance:

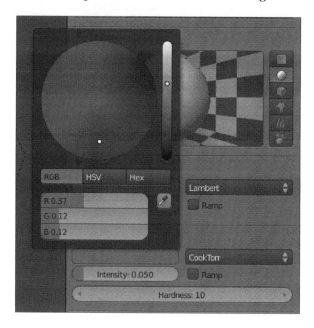

That's it! Let's render our image to check on our progress.

It's coming along quite nicely! Next, we're going to tackle the lampshades on the hanging lamps.

Giving our lampshades some color

This is going to be a pretty straightforward material. To start, we need to give it a color. For now, let's give it a sandy color to compliment the color of the walls.

1. Add a new material and name it `lampshade`.

2. Change the diffuse color to a sandy color—refer to the image below for help.

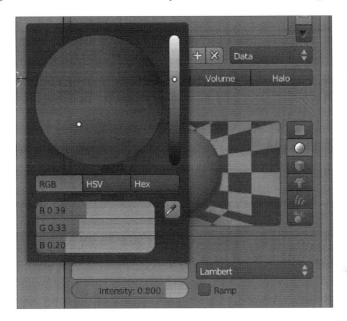

Next, we're going to adjust the specular properties.

3. Change the specular color to a light, desaturated yellow.

4. Change the **Intensity** to `0.436`.

5. Change the **Hardness** to `10`.

   Because lampshades typically get a lot of backlighting from being so close to the lamp's light source, we need to adjust the **Translucency** value to simulate that effect.

6. Set the **Translucency** value to `0.435`—this should be perfect for what we're going for.

   For our lampshade, we're going to use one of Blender's procedural textures to give our surface a little offset.

7. Under the **Textures** menu, create a new texture, naming it `lampshade_bump`.

    We're going to use the default **Cloud** texture Blender provides us, but we're going to change the settings a bit.

8. Change the **Size** to `0.05` and the **Depth** to `6`.

    Changing the **Size** value will make our texture more condensed, while the **Depth** value with give it more detail.

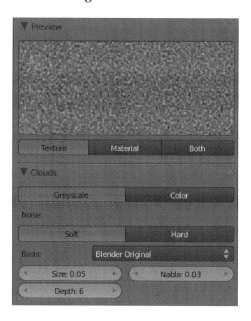

    Finally, we have to tell Blender to use the texture as a bump map, not a color map.

9. Under the **Influence** settings, uncheck the box next to **Color**, and check the box next to **Normal**.

10. Change the **Normal** value to `0.05`—because we don't want the texture to greatly affect the mesh, we need to set the value relatively low.

Next, we have to turn on transparency for our lampshade material. To do this:

1. Activate the **Transparency** settings.

2. Set the **Transparency** to **Raytrace**.

3. Set the **IOR** value to `1.55`.

4. Set the **Fresnel** to `1.0`.

5. Finally, set the **Gloss** value to `0.9`.

Let's render our image one more time to check on our progress.

It's not perfect, but it'll do for now—we may end up coming back and tweaking it later. For now, let's finish up adding materials to those lamps.

Now, select the object named `lamp_cover` and then:

1. Add a new material named `metal`.

2. Add a new texture named `metal_bump`.

3. Load the `metal_bump.png` image from the `images` folder.

4. Deselect **Color** under the **Influence** settings.

5. Select **Normal** and set the **Normal** value to `0.3`.

6. Under the **Materials** menu, change the diffuse color to a light brown, as shown in the following image:

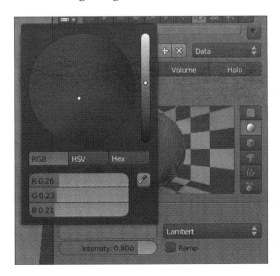

Change the specular color to off-white. Also, set the **Intensity** to 0.697 and the **Hardness** to 250. Because this is a metal texture, we want the specular values to be high.

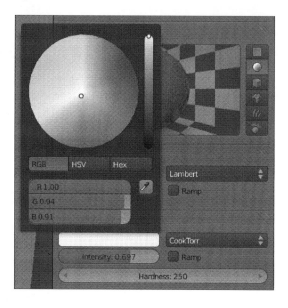

Next, we're going to adjust the **Mirror** settings. Select the checkbox next to the **Mirror** heading to activate the reflection settings. Set the **Reflectivity** setting to 0.2—we don't want a lot of reflection, but enough to notice in the render. Bump up the **Fresnel** value to 2.0 as well. Finally, set the **Depth** setting to 6 to add a little extra detail to the reflections.

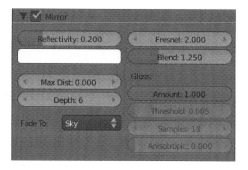

Add our metal material to the following objects:

- lamp_cover
- lamp_arm
- lamp_base

There we have it! Let's do another render.

Great! Let's finish up the lamps by adding a material to the light bulbs.

Turning on the lights

This material will be similar to the last one in many ways. Start by selecting one of the light bulbs and adding a new material. Name it light_bulb and change the diffuse color to a light yellow.

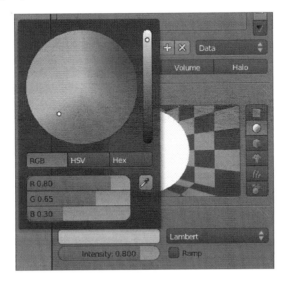

Next, change the specular color to an even lighter yellow, and set the intensity up to `0.780`. Also, set the **Hardness** to `250`. This will help create the "shiny" effect of the light bulb. Then, turn on the **Mirror** settings and set **Reflectivity** to `0.2`. Also, set the **Fresnel** to `1.0` and the **Depth** to `6`. Finally, we need our light bulb to appear as if it's emitting light. Underneath the **Shading** settings, turn up the **Emit** value to `2.0`. That's it! Once again, do another render to see how we're doing.

Looking good! There's one last material we need to add — the material for the remaining tables.

Adding the final wood material

Because we already created the material for the booths earlier, we can just use the same one for the tables as well. Add the material `booth_wood` to the following objects:

- `table_top`
- `table_leg`
- `table_top.001`
- `table_leg.001`

Also, notice how the rim light on our wine bottle doesn't feel natural. This is because the rim looks white, and there are no white light sources in our scene. Because the yellow hanging lamps would affect the rim color, change the color of the rim lamp we created to a light yellow hue.

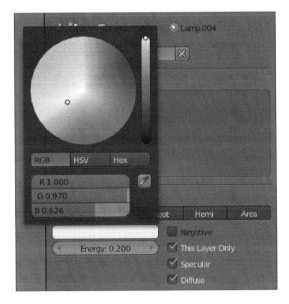

Now we can render out our image again!

For dramatic effect

Our scene is almost done! For dramatic effect, we're going to add a depth of field aspect to our render, so our wine bottle really pops from the background. To do this, we need to select our camera and adjust some settings.

With our camera selected, go into the **Camera** settings and find the **Depth of Field** textbox. Because we want the scene to focus on the wine bottle, type `wine_bottle` into the textbox. This tells Blender to focus on the wine bottle during a render.

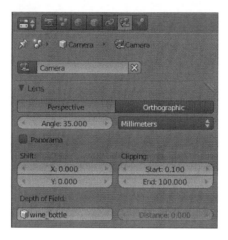

We're not quite done yet. We need to use Blender's node compositor to finish this off. Remember when we changed interface layouts to work on our UV map? We're going to do that again, but instead, we're going to use the Compositing layout. Switch to the Compositing layout and we'll get started.

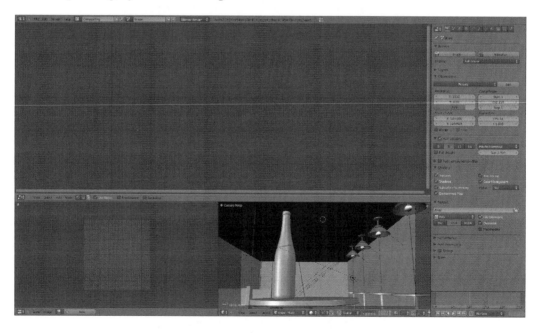

To start, we need to tell Blender that we'll be using nodes in our render. To do this, select the checkbox next to the **Use Nodes** option.

Add a new Render Layer node by selecting **Add | Input | Render Layers**. To blur our image, we're going to use our image's Z channel (dictated by the focal distance we set earlier) and a Defocus node. Add a Defocus node by going to **Add | Filter | Defocus**. We're going to want to hook up the Z-output of the Render Layer to the Z-input of the Defocus node in addition to the Image-output to input connection.

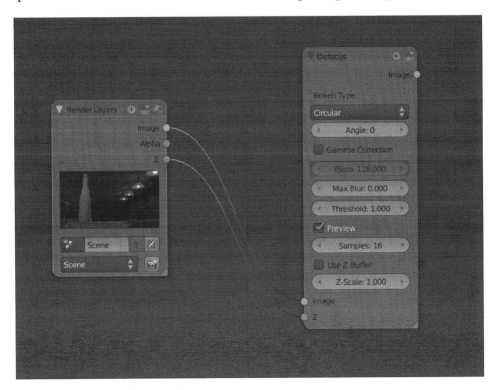

Make sure that we deselect the **Preview** option and select **Use Z-Buffer** instead. This will activate the **fStop** option, which dictates how blurry our image will be. Change the **fStop** value to 10.0 (the lower the value, the more blurry the image will be).

Next, we need to tell Blender to send this information to the renderer. To do this, we need a Composite node. Add one by selecting **Add | Output | Composite**.

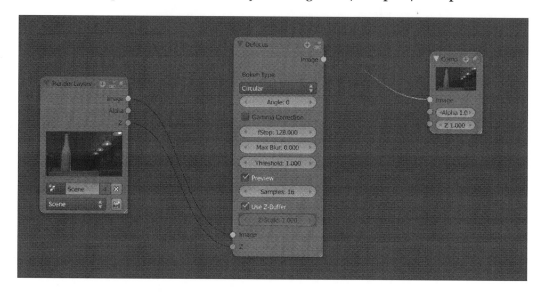

Finally, under the **World** menu, select **Full Sample** underneath the **Antialiasing** settings. This will create a nice smooth transition between the parts of the scene that are in focus and the parts of the scene that aren't. That's it! We can render out our image now!

We're done! It's been a long journey but we've finally finished this scene!

Summary

Congratulations! We've successfully completed the second project! It's been tough and we've talked about a lot of new topics on the way. We've discussed:

- Adding textures to materials
- Marking UV seams
- Unwrapping and exporting UV coordinates
- Using GIMP to create a custom UVmap
- Applying UV maps to meshes
- Using Blender's displacement feature
- Basic use of Blender's node compositor and using it to enhance our scene

We've taken a look at lighting and texturing both outdoor and indoor environments. Next, we're going to take a look at a scene that incorporates elements of both environments and what we should consider in those situations. Onto the next!

8
Combining Indoor and Outdoor Lighting Techniques

Knowing how to set up lights to use in both purely indoor and purely outdoor scenes is an essential foundation to lighting all kinds of environments. Many situations, though, aren't entirely in one specific type of lighting environment. As a result, we have to know how to incorporate both indoor as well as outdoor techniques to a single scene, as well as what traits of each style should be, and shouldn't be, included when we light our scene.

We've also taken a look at the different ways of mentally approaching these scenes. For hybrid lighting styles, we should forget what we have talked about concerning light rigs and how to strictly obey those rules of lighting, and lighting in a more interactive nature with our environments.

We're going to light an indoor porch, similar to the preceding image, while discussing:

- What kind of environments require multiple styles of lighting
- How we should mentally approach our scenarios
- What aspects of each style are important, and what can be left out

Downloading the files

Before we get started, as usual, we should make sure that we have the proper files we need to light our scene. For now, we just need the blend file `porch.blend`, which we can download from this book's resource page at `http://www.cgshark.com/lighting-and-rendering/`.

Hybrid lighting in the real world

Although it's possible to find real situations that are only lit through one style of lighting (indoor vs. outdoor), it's much more common to come across environments that are affected by light from both areas to different degrees. This can include a garage with the door left open, the underside of a bridge, or the overhang in front of a building.

The following is an example of an environment lit by both artificial and natural light sources:

Erin `http://www.flickr.com/photos/character/4244611051/sizes/z/`

Finding the right mix

The first thing we notice about scenes like the garage in the image above is that ambient light plays a larger role in lighting the environment than the actual physical light sources do. As we're used to lighting with direct light sources (such as hanging lamps), we need to change our mental approach to these scenes.

Changing our mindset

Previously, we focused on how we can use our light rigs either separately or in combination with each other to light our scenes. With "hybrid" lighting, we don't have to follow those rules as strictly as we had in the past. As we're going to rely on ambient light to flood our scene with light and color, we can focus more on where light is physically coming from in our scene, instead of how we can use rigs to simulate where light is coming from. This means that for every physical light source that will affect how our scene looks, we should place a 3D lamp that closely mimics the physical light's properties. In the end, we will have a scene that has just as many 3D lamps in the scene as there are light sources—with a couple of exceptions, which we will discuss later.

So, at least for the first part of this project, we can completely forget everything we've learned about light rigs and just focus on our scene. Some questions we will ask ourselves are:

- Where is light physically coming from?
- How many lights will we need to effectively simulate this lighting environment?
- What parts of the scene will be lit by ambient light?

Take a minute and open up our `porch.blend` file. If you downloaded the right version, you should see something similar to the image below:

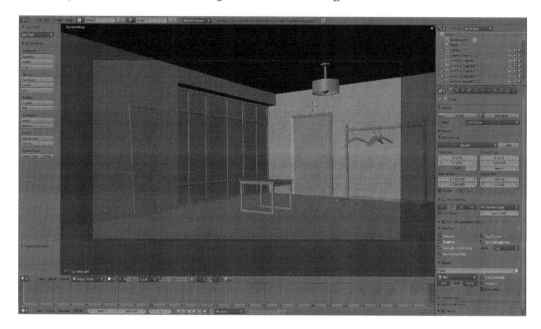

For this scene, there are really only two sources of light—the sun coming through the window and the lamp hanging from the ceiling. We're going to let the remainder of the scene be lit by ambient light, so there's no need to simulate that with a light rig. As the light bulb is modeled and visible from our camera's viewpoint, we're going to need to set up a little "mini" rig to make the lamp appear to work correctly—we can use a setup similar to the one we made for the hanging lamps in our indoor scene. So, including the lights needed for the lamp, we're only going to need three lamps for our scene. Seems simple enough, right?

Lighting the scene

We have a solid idea of where light is coming from and how it should act in our scene, so the next step is to jump right in and light it. We can start by playing with the light coming from the sun and sky through the window. In the past, we've used a Sun lamp to simulate sunlight. However, this time, we're going to do something slightly different. The main reason for this is that light bounces.

For example, imagine we're in a well-lit hallway and we open a door leading to an unlit room. Although there are corners and niches of the room that the light from the hallway isn't directly hitting, we would still be able to see most of what's in the room just from standing in the doorway.

The following image is an example of indirect lighting:

Adding sunlight

Let's return to our scene. The reason we're not using a Sun lamp to simulate the sunlight is because we need to produce nice, soft shadows in our render, which are a characteristic of shadows cast by indirect light coming from the sky. To do this:

1. Add an Area lamp.

2. Position it using either the *G-hotkey* or the Transform Widget until it is outside of the window, facing our room.

3. Change the Area Shape to Rectangle.

4. Set the Size X value to `1.0` and the Size Y value to `3.0`.

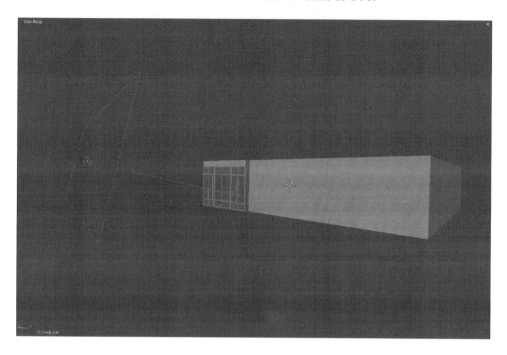

5. By default, the Area lamp's Distance value is set to `25`. For our purposes, we can set it to `3.84`.

6. Set the **Shadow** type to **Ray Shadow**

7. Set the **Samples** value to `16` for both X and Y.

This will increase the shadow quality.

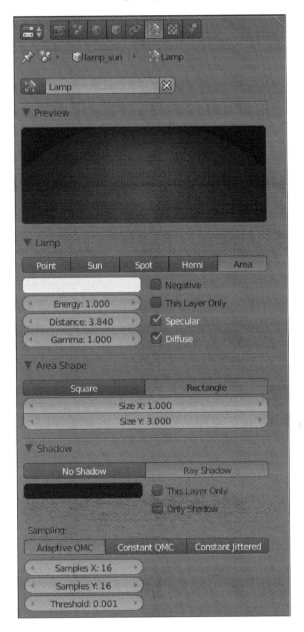

The next step is to set the lamp's color. As a good majority of the light coming through the window will be coming from the sky, we'll give the lamp a slight blue hue to create the illusion that the light is coming from the sky.

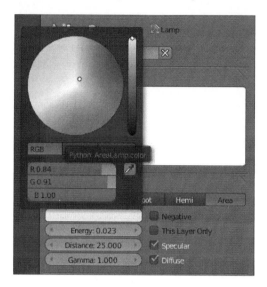

Let's do a quick test render to see what this light does to our scene.

It's looking pretty good—we'll tackle those dark spots in a moment. Purely for comparison's sake, this following image is the same render, but the Area lamp has been replaced with a Sun lamp. Notice how the light works in a very strict, linear fashion, which, although looks cool, isn't the effect we're looking for.

Playing with ambient light

Remember when we used the **Environment Lighting** settings in our indoor scene to lighten up some of the dark areas of the room? We're going to do the same here to eliminate those unrealistically dark shadows in our current scene.

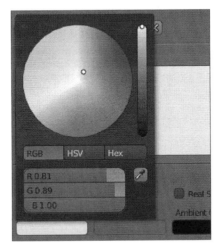

1. Under the **World** settings, change Horizon Color to a slight blue hue. We'll use this in conjunction with our Environment Lighting settings to light our room.

 Why a blue color? We're giving our world a blue horizon color because the sky primarily emits blue light. For the same reason we chose to give our Area lamp a blue hue, we're giving our ambient light a blue hue to match the color values and give our render a consistent look.

2. Activate the **Environment Lighting** settings further down in the menu by selecting the checkbox next to the settings header.

3. Bump up the Energy value to 0.3.

   By default, Blender uses white as the **Environment Lighting** color. We need to tell Blender to use our **World** settings instead, so go to the next step.

4. Underneath the **Environment Lighting** settings, select the **Sky Color** option from the list of color sources.

5. Further down in the menu, under the **Gather** options, choose the Approximate algorithm, and increase the number of Passes to 5. This will give us a better ambient occlusion calculation than we would get with the default settings.

Let's do another quick render and see how we're doing! We should now be able to see the entire room.

That looks so much better! Believe it or not, we're almost done with lighting this scene. The next step is to construct that "mini" rig for the hanging lamp and then we can move on and add materials and textures!

Organization is key

Just like we did with the hanging lamps in our indoor lighting project, we're going to need to place the different parts of the hanging lamp on separate layers so that we can light them properly.

Let's think about this conceptually for a minute. We need one lamp to illuminate our room in general. But, because of the way Blender renders light interacting with 3D meshes, we are going to need to place the lampshade, the light bulb, and the interior parts of the lampshade on another layer.

In addition, we need to illuminate the interior of the lampshade. This means we need to create another lamp and place it on the same layer as the meshes we just moved. But, again, we don't want the light bulb mesh to occlude that lamp either, so to fix that, we should move the light bulb mesh again to yet another layer.

Seems confusing? Let's construct it together and see how this will work in practice.

Constructing our "mini" rig

First, we need to move our meshes so that they're on specific layers. To do this, select the meshes named:

- lamp_shade
- lamp_support01
- lamp_support02
- lamp_screw01
- lamp_screw02
- lamp_screw03
- lamp_screw04
- lamp_lightbulb

Move all of these meshes onto Layer 2 by pressing the *M-hotkey* and select the second layer button. Now we can set the first lamp where the lamp shade used to be on Layer 1.

1. Make sure that Layer 1 is selected and add a Point lamp by selecting **Add | Lamp | Point**.

2. Position it using the *G-hotkey* or the Transform Widget so that it's in the same position as the lampshade (and the other components we just moved). Under the **Lamp** settings, change the color to a yellow hue — to simulate the color of an artificial incandescent bulb — and lower the Energy value to 0.8.

3. Make sure the **This Layer Only** option is selected. This is an important key to getting our light rig to work properly.

The following is a screenshot of the Color settings for Point Lamp:

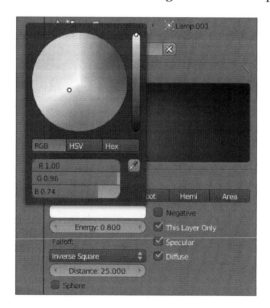

The next step is to duplicate this lamp so that we can illuminate the other parts of the lamp on Layer 2. To do this:

1. Duplicate the lamp by pressing *Shift-D*. Confirm the duplication with a left mouse click.

2. With the newly duplicated lamp still selected, move it to Layer 2 using the *M-hotkey*. We're going to need to modify some of the settings of the new lamp, so navigate to the second layer and make sure our new lamp is still selected.

3. Increase the Energy value of our new lamp to 1.5. Also make sure that the **This Layer Only** option is still selected.

Finally, we need to move our light bulb so that it doesn't occlude the light from our newly duplicated lamp. Select the `lamp_lightbulb` mesh and move it to the third layer using the *M-hotkey*.

That's it! We've done it! Let's do one final render to see how our scene now looks.

Summary

Lighting environments with both artificial and natural light sources isn't easy, but as we've learned, this can be achieved by breaking it down and changing our approach a bit. We now know that although it's essential to know about how to use generic light rigs, sometimes the best thing to do is to just think about how our scene is set up and try to simulate lighting our scene that way. We've also talked about:

- Various real-world environments that are lit by both natural and artificial light sources

- How to simulate light *bending* with 3D lighting techniques

- How to use ambient light to illuminate dark corners and crevices in our scene

- How to set up a small *rig* to create the illusion that our hanging lamp is functional and turned on

- How to simulate how color will affect our scene by changing the World and Lamp color values

That lighting setup was easy enough once we broke it down, wasn't it? Now we can move on to adding materials and textures!

9
Hybrid Lighting: Materials and Textures

We've already taken an in-depth look at a lot of different techniques that we can use to make our materials look believable, including:

- Adjusting diffuse and specular settings
- Adding reflections and transparency
- Using image textures as UV maps

Now we're going to focus on bringing those materials to the next level and really take a look at what we can do to mimic real-life objects.

Downloading the files

As always, let's grab the files we're going to use for this project. To download the proper files, visit `http://www.cgshark.com/lighting-and-rendering/` and download the project file `hybrid.zip`. This ZIP file contains our pre-compiled project folder with the following images:

- `room_color.png`
- `tabletop.png`
- `wood_yellow.png`
- `wood_brown.png`
- `metal.png`

We're going to use these images with our materials for this scene.

Referencing real-world images

This scene will require a lot of UV mapping, but all of that work has been done ahead of time, giving us leeway to really work our materials out. We're going to take a look at each material individually and compare our 3D materials with our reference image as well as real-life examples of objects with similar properties. Let's get started!

Referring to our reference image

It's always important to have a reference image (or images) to use when working in 3D. Because our scene is nearly a direct copy of our reference image, it's extremely useful to continually refer to it for guidance.

On its own, this room has a lot of objects with unique looks that we'll want to simulate in our own scene. The walls of the room, the glossiness of the table, the reflections in the mirror—we're going to have to set all of those values separately in our scene to create a believable effect.

The room material

The biggest and most noticeable aspect of the room is the boundaries of the room itself. This includes the walls, ceiling, and floor of our scene. Now, our scene is pretty large already, and because the boundaries of our room take up most of the scene, we're going to need a fairly large image to get the proper texture quality in our final render—we don't need our textures pixelating (or distorting) in our final render.

Because the UV map was already made ready-to-use for us, we can just load it into Blender right away. First, we should add the texture that defines the overall color and texture our room will have. Let's set up the basic material. To do this:

1. Select the object labeled `room`.

2. Add a new material under the **Material** menu.

3. Rename the new material to `room_MAT`.

4. Under the `Specular` settings, set the **Hardness** to `20`.

Simple enough—now that our material is all set, we can bring our first texture into Blender. To do this:

1. Navigate to the **Texture** menu and create a new texture.

2. Rename the new texture to `room_color`.

3. Change the texture Type to **Image or Movie** and browse for the texture file named `room_color.png`.

 Assuming the project folder is named `porch`, the texture will be found under `porch/textures/room_color.png`.

4. Under the **Mapping** settings, change the Coordinates to UV and set the UV layer to UVTex. This will tell Blender to look at the UV coordinates of our room, instead of the default coordinates generated by Blender.

Let's do a quick render to see how our scene looks.

For a first render, that's looking pretty good. There are still some issues with the specular values, though, so let's tackle that next. We can use another texture to define what sections of the room we want to have a specular value and what areas we don't want. For example, in our reference image, there's a specular shine on the floor of the room, but not so much on the walls or ceiling. We can use a texture to define what areas are specular and which ones aren't.

1. With the room still selected, go back to the **Textures** menu and create another texture.

2. Rename the texture `room_spec`.

3. Following the steps on the previous page, change the texture Type to **Image or Movie** and adjust the Mapping values to UV.

4. Load the image file named `room_specular.png`. It's found under the `textures` folder in the `project` folder.

5. Underneath the **Influence** settings, unselect the currently selected **Color** option and instead select the **Intensity and Color** values under the **Specular** options.

6. Under the material's **Specular** settings, change the Intensity to `0.0`. We're doing this because we want the texture to affect the specularity, not the default values.

We also want to use this texture to affect the reflections on our floor. To do this:

1. Go back to the **Material** menu and enable the **Mirror settings**.

2. Set the **Fresnel** value to `5.0`.

3. Change the **Depth** value to `6`.

Return to the **Texture** menu and perform the following:

1. Under the `room_spec` texture's **Influence** settings, activate the **Mirror** and **Ray Mirror** settings. This will tell Blender to use the texture with the Mirror values.

2. Set the **Ray Mirror** value to `0.1`.

Let's see what changing those settings did to our render:

That looks a lot better! Now that the main part of the room is done, let's take a look at the block above the window. We need to create a concrete texture to apply to this object so that it matches the ceiling. To do this:

1. Select the cube named `overhang`.

2. Create a new material. Name it `concrete_MAT`.

3. Under the **Specular** settings, change the **Intensity** to `0.2` and the **Hardness** to `10`.

 Although concrete is, in real-life, a hard material, its specular is soft in comparison to other materials like glass or some plastics. Don't confuse the Hardness value of the material's Specular value with the hardness of the object itself!

4. Create a new texture and name it `concrete_color`.

5. We don't need to use UV-coordinates for this material, so just change the **Project type** to `Cube`.

6. Under the **Influence** settings, select the **Normal** option (in addition to the already selected **Color** option) and set the value to `0.5`.

That should be good! Let's just make sure it looks okay in the render before we move on.

That'll work! Now let's take a look at the mirror leaning against the brick wall.

The mirror material

The mirror is a relatively easy material to simulate. Let's start with the main part of the mirror—the reflective material.

1. Select the object named `mirror_glass`.

2. Create a new material. Name it `mirror_MAT`.

3. Set the **Specular Intensity** to `0.719`

4. Set the **Hardness** to `100`.

5. Turn on Mirror reflections and change the **Reflectivity** value to `1.0`. This will create the mirror effect.

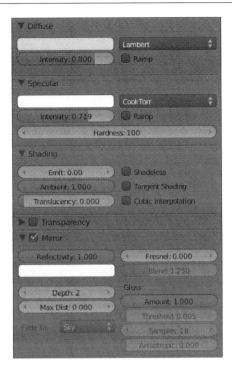

As we've discussed, no material is a *perfect* material. This means that even the smoothest surfaces have small imperfections in them. We can use a texture to add some bumps to our mirror to *break* the smooth look of the mirror slightly. To add the bump map

6. With the glass still selected, add a new texture and name it `mirror_bump`.

7. Change the **Texture** Type to **Wood**.

8. Under the Influence settings, deselect the **Color** option, and select the **Normal** option. Set the value to `0.01`.

While we're at it, we can add the material for the wood frame on the mirror as well. To do this:

9. Select one of the frame's edges and add a new material.

10. Rename the newly created material to `mirrorframe_MAT`.

11. Set the **Specular Intensity** to `0.15` and the **Hardness** to `20`. This will give the wood a nice, soft look.

12. Switch over to the **Texture** menu and add a new Image or Movie texture. Load the texture named `wood_brown.png`, which is found under our `textures` folder.

13. Set the project type to **Cube**.

That's it! Now, add our wood material to the rest of the frame by selecting the other frame sides one at a time and adding the material from the current materials list in the **Material** menu. We can even use it for the window frames! Select the following objects and apply the `mirrorframe_MAT` material to them:

- `window_topframe`
- `window_bottomframe`
- `windowL_leftframe`
- `windowL_innerframe`

- windowL_rightframe
- windowC_leftframe
- windowC_innerframe
- windowC_rightframe
- windowR_leftframe
- windowR_innerframe
- windowR_rightframe

Let's do another render to see how we're doing.

Great! Let's keep going. We'll just keep moving right in our scene and tackle the table next.

The table material

The table really comprises two materials—a black metal texture for the base and legs and a UV texture for the tabletop. We're going to work with the metallic texture first. With the table legs selected (table_legs):

1. Create a new material, naming it black_metal_MAT.

2. Adjust the Diffuse color to a gray color. Look at the following image for help:

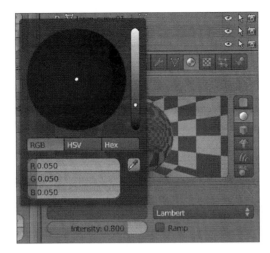

3. Turn up the **Hardness** value to 300. Remember, a higher Hardness value means a smaller specular shine, which creates the illusion of a harder surface.

   Also, remember that most metallic materials have some degree of reflection, so we're going to need to play with the **Mirror** settings.

4. Activate the **Mirror** settings.

5. Set the **Reflectivity** value to 0.3.

6. The **Fresnel** value to 2.0.

7. The **Gloss Amount** to 0.97. This is important because our reflections will appear blurry.

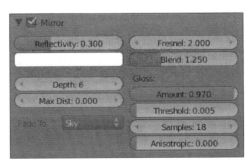

That's it! Select the object named `table_base` and add the metal texture to it as well. Now let's move on to the tabletop. The tabletop material is made up of a pre-mapped UV-texture, found in the `textures` folder of the project directory. With the tabletop selected, carry out the following steps:

1. Add a new material, naming it `tabletop_MAT`.

2. Set the **Specular Intensity** to `0.644`, and the Hardness to `20`.

   We're also going to want a slight reflection off the top of this table as well, so we need to activate the **Mirror** settings again.

3. Set the **Reflectivity** value to `0.02`, and the **Gloss** Amount to `0.9`. This will really blur the reflections to a point where the reflections are indistinguishable.

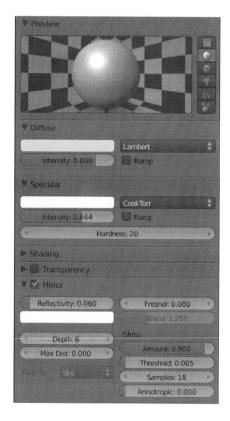

Now we need to add the UV map to give our tabletop some color. In the Textures menu:

1. Add a new texture, naming it `tabletop_color`.

2. Set the Type to **Image or Movie**, and load the UV-texture named `tabletop_color.png`.

3. Under the **Mapping** settings, change the Coordinates to UV and select the **UVTex** layer.

That should do it! Let's do another render and see how our scene is turning out.

Not too bad! Let's keep going. The next step is the door.

The door material

The door will be quite similar to the other wood material we made — the only difference is the color of the wood. We can start by selecting the door and adding the existing material named `mirrorframe_MAT`.

1. With the object selected, press the button with the number directly to the right of the material name (under the **Material** menu) to make a single-user copy. Refer to the following image for help:

2. Rename the material to `door_MAT`.

3. Under the textures menu, make the texture a single-user copy as well. Blender treats textures as separate entities from materials, so the texture wasn't duplicated when we duplicated the material.

4. Reload the image source so that Blender points to the image named
   `wood_yellow.png`.

It's that easy! Make sure the `door_MAT` material has been applied to the door and it's frame and then perform another render. We're getting there!

Looking good! Let's move on to the hanging lamp now.

The hanging light materials

The hanging lamp consists of multiple materials, including a material for the light bulb, a material for the lampshade, and a material for the metal support the light is hanging from. Let's begin with the light bulb. To create the material for the light bulb

1. Select the object named `light_bulb` and add a new material.

2. Name our new material `lightbulb_MAT`.

3. Change the diffuse color to a yellow hue. Refer to the image below:

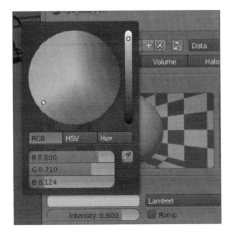

4. Set the emit value to `1.10`. This will make the light bulb appear to emit light.

   Now let's look at the lampshade. Remember when we had to play with the material settings in our indoor scene to make the lampshades look as if there were being illuminated from the back? We're going to do the same here to simulate the same effect.

5. Select the lampshade.

6. Create a new material named `lampshade_MAT`.

7. Change the diffuse Color to a beige shade – refer to the following image for help:

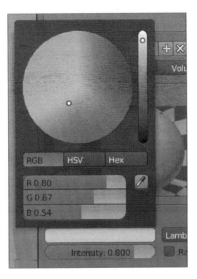

8. Under the **Specular** settings, set the color value to an off-white hue.

9. Set the **Hardness** value to 200.

10. Under the **Shading** settings, there's an option called **Translucency**. Set its value to 0.7.

11. Turn on the **Transparency** options, and set the algorithm to **Raytrace**.

12. Set the **Fresnel** to 1.0.

13. Set the **IOR** value to 1.55. This is the average IOR value of most commercial glass products.

14. We're going to want to blur the transparency values as well, so change the **Gloss Amount** value to 0.95.

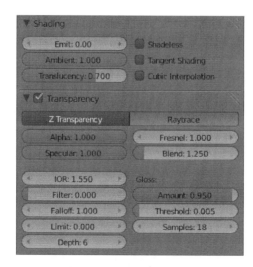

Now we just need to take a look at the metal texture, which we will use for many of the remaining objects in our scene. Start by selecting the object named `lamp_base`, and:

1. Add a new material named `brushed_metal_MAT`.

2. Set the diffuse Color to a light gray. Refer to the image below for help:

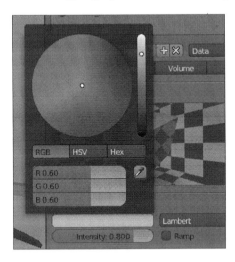

3. Set the **Hardness** value to `300`.

4. Turn on the **Mirror** settings.

5. Set the **Reflectivity** value to `0.02`.

Now we just need to add our bump map, giving the texture a *brushed* feel. Under the **Textures** menu:

1. Add a new image texture and name it `brushed_metal_bump`.

2. Load the image named `brushed_metal.png`.

3. Under the **Mapping** settings, change the Projection to Cube.

4. Under the **Influence** settings, set the Normal value to `1.0`.

Now we just need to add this material to the rest of the objects. Take the next couple of minutes to add the newly-created metal material to the following objects:

- `lamp_arm`
- `coatrack_top`
- `coatrack_base`
- `coatrack_support01`
- `coatrack_support02`

- hanger01_hook
- hanger02_hook
- hanger03_hook

We've made a lot of changes—let's render out our image and see how it looks.

We're almost done—one more material to go! We need to create the plastic material that we'll use on the coat hangers and the feet of the coat rack.

The coat hanger material

If you take a look at any coat hanger with a plastic base, you'll probably notice that there are tiny bumps and imperfections in the material. As with many other materials we made, we're going to apply the same effect to our plastic material.

1. Select any of the coat hangers and add a new material.
2. Rename the new material to black_plastic_MAT.

3. Set the diffuse Color to an off-black shade. Refer to the image below for more information:

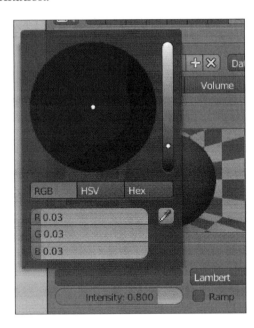

4. Under the **Specular** settings, set the Color value to a medium gray value (refer to the image below):

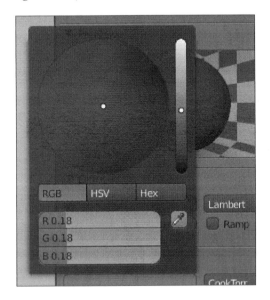

5. Set the **Intensity** to `0.151`.

6. Set the **Hardness** to `20`.

Now we can create the texture!

1. Create a new Cloud texture and name it `plastic_bump`.

2. Set the **Size** to `0.02` and the **Nabla** to `0.03`.

3. Under the **Influence** settings, deselect the **Color** option, and select the Normal option.

4. Set the **Normal** value to `0.1`.

That's it! Now, we just need to add the material to the following objects:

* `hanger01_base`
* `hanger02_base`
* `hanger03_base`
* `coatrack_legpad01`
* `coatrack_legpad02`
* `coatrack_legpad03`
* `coatrack_legpad04`

That's it! Let's perform one final render.

Summary

This has been one intense project. We've talked about lighting techniques used in hybrid lighting scenes, including when to use ambient light to light a scene in comparison to direct light. We've also taken a look at many different materials with varying properties, including:

- Plastic
- Metal
- Glass
- Wood
- Brick
- Marble
- Concrete

That's a lot! The key to making each one work is to try to simulate how it may actually work in real life. Sounds obvious, but many users forget when the time comes to actually make the materials. Good luck blending!

Index

G

general rig
area lamps, setting up 112-116
setting up 101
spot lamps, adding 101-105
Geometry node
creating 171
G-hotkey 102
G-Hotkey 110, 127
GIMP
downloading 137
Hello GIMP! 137, 138
glass material
Alpha input 159
compositing layout 155
Depth parameter 160
Fresnel value, editing 158
glass Material node 157
Gloss parameter 160
Gloss value 160
Material node 156
New button 156
new material, creating 155
node network 156
reflections, adding 161
glass material node 157, 168
Global illumination (GI). *See* **also**
ambient lighting
Gloss parameter 80, 160
Guide
creating 144, 145

H

halo material type 72, 73
hanging light materials
about 218-221
bump map, adding 221
material, creating for light bulb 218-221
materials, adding to objects 221, 222
HDR
about 59
used, for lighting scene 60-64
Height attribute 138
hemi lamp 20, 91

Henrietta text layer
duplicating 147
High Dynamic Range. *See* **HDR**
hybrid lighting 192
hybrid.zip
downloading 205

I

images
downloading 174
incandescent light bulbs 12
Index of Refraction (IOR) 78
indirect lighting
about 64
ambient lighting, applying to working
scene 65
approximate indirect lighting algorithm 64
example 195
indoor lighting
about 193
setting up 97
indoor_lighting folder 154
indoor_lights.blend
URL, for downloading 121
influence settings 54
interface
changing 122, 123
interior.blend file
website, for downloading 97
Interior Lighting download section 97
Interpolation 77

K

key light 23, 41, 92

L

label_image texture 171
label_image Texture node 172
label_mask texture 171
label_mask Texture node 172
label material
Add | Color | Mix 167
Compositing screen layout 170
creating 164
Geometry node, creating 171

R

Ray Shadow 111
raytraced ambient lighting algorithm 50
raytraced ambient occlusion
  about 50, 93
  advantages 57
  disadvantages 57
raytraced shadow 29
raytraced transparency 77
realistic lighting 7
realistic result 158
real-world images
  referencing 206
reference image
  getting 138, 140
  referencing 206
  referring to 206
  using 133-135
reflections, adding to glass
  Diffuse settings 162
  Fresnel parameter 164
  Specular settings 162, 163
  steps 161
render
  enhancing, layers used 98
rendering 32
render settings, Blender
  scene menu 32
R-Hotkey 127
rim light *See* backlight
room material
  about 206-210
  basic material, setting up 206
  texture menu 208
rubber material
  burning 84, 85

S

Sample Buffers setting 107
sampling setting, ambient occlusion
  about 53
  new settings 56
Scalable Vector Graphic (SVG) 138
Scale Tool 150
scene
  3-Point light rig, setting up 40-42

3-Point light rig used 38
  backlight, dimensionality adding with 46
  downloading, URL 31
  evaluating 36, 37, 90
  fill light, adding 46
  hybrid scene 31
  indoor scene 31
  lamp color, adjusting 42
  lamp menu 43
  lighting 194
  light rig, planning 38, 39
  materials, creating for 81-84
  outdoor scene 31
  setting up 39, 40
  shadows, adding 45
  workflow, establishing 36
  working with 31
scene, lighting
  about 194
  ambient light 199, 200
  mini rig, constructing 201, 202
  sunlight, adding 195-199
scene menu, render settings
  about 32
  dimension settings 35
  output settings 35, 36
  render settings 32-35
seam
  creating 124
  marking 123
secondary colors 8
Shadeless 76
shading settings
  about 76
  Ambient 76
  Emit 76
  interpolation 77
  shadeless 76
  tangent shading 77
  Translucency 76
shadows
  adding 45
  enabling 45
Shadow settings 108
S-Hotkey 127
single-user copy
  creating 86, 87

Size 106
specular 74
Specular color 163
Specular settings 162
specular shader models 75
sphere projection 123
spot lamps
  about 18, 19, 91
  adding 101, 106-112
Spot Shape settings 106
Standard rig 26, 28
Studio rig 26, 27
sun lamp 16, 17
sunlight
  adding, to scene 195-199
surface material type 70

T

table material
  about 214-217
  black metal texture 214
  tabletop, selecting 215
  UV-map, adding to tabletop 216
  UV texture 214
Tangent Shading 77
tertiary colors 9
Text tool
  using 146
Texture menu 170
Texture node 166, 167
texture seam 124
text, UV texture
  adding 144
  Guide, creating 144, 145
  Text tool, using 146
This Layer Only option 108, 110, 115, 119
Translucency 76
transparency
  ansparency 77
  depth 80
  falloff 79
  filter 79
  gloss 80
  Index of Refraction (IOR) 78
  limit 79
  settings, configuring 77
  Z Transparency 77

tricycle, material
  red plastic 87
  white plastic 87

U

U-Hotkey 125
Use Nodes option 187
UV Editing layout 122, 123
UV_help.jpg texture
  URL, for downloading 134
UV map
  cleaning 126-128
  exporting 136, 137, 154
  importing 140-144
  rotating 126
  UV editing tools 129-133
UV texture
  creating 135, 136
  GIMP, downloading 137
  Hello GIMP! 137, 138
  reference images, getting 138, 139
  Save often! 146
  text, adding 144, 145, 146
  UV map, exporting 136, 137
  UV map, importing 140-144

V

volume material type 71, 72

W

wallpaper
  adding 177-179
Width attribute 138
wine bottle
  lighting 117, 119
wire material type 70
wood material
  adding 175
  creating 174
  mapping projection type, changing 175
  Preview mesh 175
  render, testing 176
  wood material, adding 184, 185

Thank you for buying
Blender 2.5 Lighting and Rendering

About Packt Publishing

Packt, pronounced 'packed', published its first book "*Mastering phpMyAdmin for Effective MySQL Management*" in April 2004 and subsequently continued to specialize in publishing highly focused books on specific technologies and solutions.

Our books and publications share the experiences of your fellow IT professionals in adapting and customizing today's systems, applications, and frameworks. Our solution based books give you the knowledge and power to customize the software and technologies you're using to get the job done. Packt books are more specific and less general than the IT books you have seen in the past. Our unique business model allows us to bring you more focused information, giving you more of what you need to know, and less of what you don't.

Packt is a modern, yet unique publishing company, which focuses on producing quality, cutting-edge books for communities of developers, administrators, and newbies alike. For more information, please visit our website: www.packtpub.com.

About Packt Open Source

In 2010, Packt launched two new brands, Packt Open Source and Packt Enterprise, in order to continue its focus on specialization. This book is part of the Packt Open Source brand, home to books published on software built around Open Source licences, and offering information to anybody from advanced developers to budding web designers. The Open Source brand also runs Packt's Open Source Royalty Scheme, by which Packt gives a royalty to each Open Source project about whose software a book is sold.

Writing for Packt

We welcome all inquiries from people who are interested in authoring. Book proposals should be sent to author@packtpub.com. If your book idea is still at an early stage and you would like to discuss it first before writing a formal book proposal, contact us; one of our commissioning editors will get in touch with you.

We're not just looking for published authors; if you have strong technical skills but no writing experience, our experienced editors can help you develop a writing career, or simply get some additional reward for your expertise.

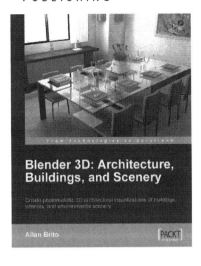

Blender 3D Architecture, Buildings, and Scenery

ISBN: 978-1-847193-67-4   Paperback: 332 pages

Create photorealistic 3D architectural visualizations of buildings, interiors, and environmental scenery

1. Turn your architectural plans into a model

2. Study modeling, materials, textures, and light basics in Blender

3. Create photo-realistic images in detail

4. Create realistic virtual tours of buildings and scenes

SketchUp 7.1 for Architectural Visualization: Beginner's Guide

ISBN: 978-1-847199-46-1   Paperback: 408 pages

Create stunning photo-realistic and artistic visuals for your SketchUp models

1. Create picture-perfect photo-realistic 3D architectural renders for your SketchUp models

2. Post-process SketchUp output to create digital watercolor and pencil art

3. Follow a professional visualization studio workflow

4. Make the most out of SketchUp with the best free plugins and add-on software to enhance your models

Please check **www.PacktPub.com** for information on our titles

JavaFX 1.2 Application Development Cookbook

ISBN: 978-1-847198-94-5   Paperback: 332 pages

Over 60 recipes to create rich Internet applications with many exciting features

1. Easily develop feature-rich internet applications to interact with the user using various built-in components of JavaFX

2. Make your application visually appealing by using various JavaFX classes—ListView, Slider, ProgressBar—to display your content and enhance its look with the help of CSS styling

3D Game Development with Microsoft Silverlight 3: Beginner's Guide

ISBN: 978-1-847198-92-1   Paperback: 452 pages

A practical guide to creating real-time responsive online 3D games in Silverlight 3 using C#, XBAP WPF, XAML, Balder, and Farseer Physics Engine

1. Develop online interactive 3D games and scenes in Microsoft Silverlight 3 and XBAP WPF

2. Integrate Balder 3D engine 1.0, Farseer Physics Engine 2.1, and advanced object-oriented techniques to simplify the game development process

Please check **www.PacktPub.com** for information on our titles

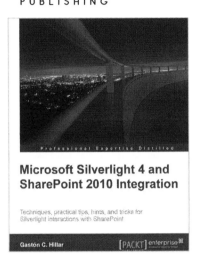
Microsoft Silverlight 4 and SharePoint 2010 Integration

ISBN: 978-1-849680-06-6   Paperback: 336 pages

Techniques, practical tips, hints, and tricks for Silverlight interactions with SharePoint

1. Develop Silverlight RIAs that interact with SharePoint 2010 data and services

2. Explore the diverse alternatives for hosting a Silverlight RIA in a SharePoint 2010 Page

3. Work with the new SharePoint Silverlight Client Object Model to interact with elements in a SharePoint Site

WordPress and Flash 10x Cookbook

ISBN: 978-1-847198-82-2   Paperback: 268 pages

Over 50 simple but incredibly effective recipes to take control of dynamic Flash content in Wordpress

1. Learn how to make your WordPress blog or website stand out with Flash

2. Embed, encode, and distribute your video content in your Wordpress site or blog

3. Build your own .swf files using various plugins

Made in the USA
Lexington, KY
20 April 2011